Ma_yh

*Is Anything
Too Hard for God?*

By the same author

Healing Revolution
Healing Secrets
The Greatest Miracle
Power for Living

Melvin Banks has ministered the Gospel for over 35 years, from the age of 17. An Assemblies of God minister, he has crusaded in some 21 nations, conducting missions and conventions and speaking in churches, chapels and fellowship groups of all denominations and backgrounds.

He has pioneered over 49 churches in Britain and Europe and has seen crowds as large as 18,000 come to his meetings.

'*From the soles of his feet to the crown of his head Melvin Banks is a pure evangelist – the works of our great God have been manifested mightily in his ministry over many years.*' **Clive Calver**

'*We commend Melvin Banks for over 30 years of outstanding ministry to the United Kingdom, turning thousands to Christ through his powerful messages of faith.*' **Dr Paul Yonggi Cho.**

The Rev. Melvin Banks would be pleased to hear from readers. Please write to him at:

Crusade Office
44 Monk's Way
Cricketts Meadow
Chippenham
Wilts
SN15 3TT
Please send s.a.e.

Tel: 0249–655712

MELVIN BANKS

Is Anything Too Hard for God?

Miraculous power for your life

Collins
Marshall Pickering

William Collins Sons & Co. Ltd
London · Glasgow · Sydney · Auckland
Toronto · Johannesburg

First published in Great Britain in 1990 by Marshall Pickering

Marshall Pickering is an imprint of
Collins Religious Division,
part of the Collins Publishing Group
8 Grafton Street, London WIX 3LA

Copyright © 1990 Melvin Banks

Printed and bound in Great Britain by William Collins
Sons & Co. Ltd, Glasgow

May McCreer

ACKNOWLEDGEMENT
To the leaders and pastors of the Assemblies of God in Great Britain, Europe and worldwide, who have personally encouraged me, over thirty years and continually opened the door that the Full Gospel might be proclaimed to multitudes. Not forgetting my many new friends in Elim, the house churches, the Baptists, and "Independent" Churches. THIS STORY IS ONLY POSSIBLE BECAUSE OF YOU!

DEDICATION
To the two women in my life, my devoted mother, Grace Banks, who bore me, taught me, loved me, prayed for me, and sacrificed a lifetime for me. To my precious darling wife Lilian Banks, the most devoted, hard working, loving partner anyone could wish for, who "burns for God" as much, if not more, than I do. They have both revealed to me and thousands that NOTHING IS TOO HARD FOR GOD.

SCRIPTURE–
"The things that mark an apostle – signs, wonders, miracles – were done among you with great perseverance . . ." (2 Cor, 12 v12). "Before the great day of the Lord, God shall turn the heart of the Fathers, and the hearts of the rebellious children . . ." (Malachi 4 vv5-6)

QUOTE–
"You cannot trust God too much" – *D. Watson.*
"All the tresaures of God and His immense power are ours through faith" – *Smith Wigglesworth.*
"This is the day of extraordinary and incredible miracles, THE HOUR OF GOD'S POWER IS HERE". – Reinhardt Bonke.

Contents

Author's Preface

Healing Revolution was a 'look-back' at my conversion to Christ, my early ministry and God's leading into the healing ministry seemingly 'by accident'. In *Is Anything Too Hard for God?* I have filled in many of the gaps not included in the former book: my early miracle of salvation from death as a child, my first tentative steps in preaching, my baptism in the Holy Ghost – a mighty experience that transformed my life and ministry. I have also brought the story up to date, with some of the latest accounts of heart-moving miracles of deliverance by the hand of Christ – sure evidences in these last days that the Spirit of God is moving amongst His Church. I have not spared some of the failures and experiences of pain in the 'house of my pilgrimage' . . . as well as referring to the great joys and victories. This book is not 'glorious triumphalism', but rather about God's extraordinary grace and His gifts through a very ordinary person with many faults and failures. I believe you will learn much about the Living Christ through this story.

PART ONE

A Life of Service

1 *Saved From Death*

I will redeem thee from the power of the grave.
                                                    – Hosea

The sun shone brightly, with not a cloud in the sky, as
Father sat basking in the deck chair. He was wheezy, but
could still smell the scent of roses on the quiet breeze, the
clear sea air of Weston-super Mare. Everywhere was still
and peaceful.

Weston might have been at peace, but the world was
not. For this was August 1940 and the war was at its
height. Even Weston was drawn in, for the beaches were
unreachable, and all you could see of the sea was barbed
wire, stern warnings to keep off the beaches, and heavy
tank defences.

Mum and Dad were still driven by a wish to get away
from it all, though, and so had hired a caravan at an all-
time low price, the only other customers being off-duty
soldiers and airmen, air wardens and WAAFs.

Father was awakened out of his dreams by the crunch
of the caravan door, and Mother appeared with a cup of
afternoon tea, the spoon betraying the presence of treacle
in the bottom of the cup: the poor man's sugar for the
next five years of the war.

'Where's Melvin?', asked Mother. 'I thought he was
out here with you.'

Dad shot to his feet. 'He was playing with our Bri'
[Brian, my brother] over there', and he pointed to a
hedgerow on the side of the camping field. There, sure
enough, was Brian: sitting on the grass, pulling up daisies
(and eating a few in the process). But no Melvin.

Suddenly Mother shuddered with horror. 'What about the stream? He didn't go down there, did he?'

Father dashed down towards the water at the bottom of the field. Mother ran off to the right to see if I had slipped under the hedge, calling to Brian to stay put. Then she too headed for the small river, the sun still shining, the birds twittering overhead. . . .

'My God, he's here!', Father cried, and leapt into the water, which came only a little above his knees. Mother could only watch, her heart thumping, as he splashed across to the motionless form, lying face down in the water.

Father grasped my body and jerked it out of the water. Holding me tight to his chest, he turned and ran back upstream, struggled up the steep bank and flung me down in the grassy field. He opened my shirt, wiped the wet from my face, shook me, tried to pump my stomach (mouth-to-mouth resuscitation was not known in those days), the tears running down his face. Minutes went by. Another neighbour from the camp site ran down and dashed off to fetch a doctor.

'It's no damned good', Father cried in despair. 'He's gone.'

Mother prayed. She stopped shrieking and said in her heart, 'God, I give him to you. Just save him.' There was silence for a few moments; no sound save the screaming of gulls high in the sky as the wind blew them across Weston Bay toward Lundy Island.

My Father, too, bent low over the lifeless body and sobbed, 'O God, O God, please God. . . .'

It was perhaps just a cry of despair, for my father was not religious and not a churchgoer, though never a complete atheist. For Mother it was different, deeper. Her own mother and grandmother had been devout believers. Her mother had been converted in the great Welsh Revival of 1904, and baptized in one of those fervent gatherings which shook Wales and brought repentance and joy to so many. Mother had been brought up strictly in the Church and had herself been converted at a Church Army evangelistic open-air service in 1928.

But she had moved away from the very religious atmosphere of the valleys, to the worldly set of South London. There she met my father, who had drifted away from the Church in the years running up to the war, and she too had slipped away from regular worship and fellowship.

Now it was all being recalled, on that grassy spot in Weston. When I stood on that spot years later, during a packed mission, I felt still a warm sense of the presence of God there.

Father let my body slide slowly down onto the grass. But suddenly he started, and cried out again, this time with excitement:

'There's breath! He's alive!'

Quickly I was wrapped in a thick blanket and towels brought by another woman from the camp site, and Father hugged the wet, shivering body to his chest. 'He's alive!' The doctor came and I was warmly wrapped up in bed in the caravan, and the next day I was normal and well.

As Mother and Father sat beside each other in the corner of the caravan, they talked into the night about the unforgettable day, constantly glancing across at their 'miracle' son. Father spoke:

'I have a strange feeling he has a special purpose in this world.'

'Yes', said Mother. 'It's as if God has spared him for. . . .' Another tear came into her eye, but she spoke with resolve. 'It's a funny, scarey feeling to have, but it's good that will come out of today.'

13

2 Punch-up in the Graveyard

... the very word is like a bell to call me back to myself...

John Keats

Lord Clive was a dissolute, lost young man, without happiness or purpose in his life. In utter despair, he pressed a gun to his head and pulled the trigger. The gun misfired. He tried again. Again nothing happened. Clive threw the gun down and declared: 'I am destined for something in life. I will find out what it is and fulfil it.' He went on to become one of the most famous governors in India, securing the jewel for the crown of the British Empire.

John Wesley knew he was saved for some purpose after he was rescued from certain death when his father's house, the Epworth parsonage, caught fire. He was a 'brand plucked from the burning' and revived English Christianity in the 18th century, travelling 250,000 miles and preaching 40,000 sermons.

John Knox also felt that God had something special for him after a bullet struck the study chair in which he had been sitting just seconds before. Later, he was largely responsible for establishing the Protestant religion in Scotland, and proved a fierce adversary to Mary Queen of Scots.

Of course my mother never thought in these terms, and neither have I. To me a special job for Jesus can be anything from washing the pots and pans to giving out the hymn books in church; from teaching each week in the Sunday School to contacting someone who is feeling discouraged.

Still, she felt that whatever was in store for her son, she was going to make sure he got the best help in preparing for it. She was determined to be true to her quiet vow, that I was to be brought up as God's own, and reasoned: mix with spiritual people, and you'll be spiritual.

That was why, at the age of seven, I stood before the towering form of the Rev Philip Snow, Vicar of Chippenham (later made a canon). His black, horn-rimmed glasses fascinated me as a child: they seemed fixed under his thick eyebrows, and I thought that he had been born with them and that they never came off! He seemed a severe figure then, but he went on to break all records as the longest-serving vicar in the town (thirty-four years). And I was saddened to hear that he had just retired when I returned to Chippenham in 1979 to set up my International Crusade office. I was never able to meet him before he died, and wish I could have told him how grateful I am for his faithfulness as a minister which helped shape my early life.

But on that first day it was joining the choir that made the greatest impact. I recall the look of indifference on the choirmaster's face as I hit notes which were certainly high, but rather out of tune. Perhaps he was used to hard cases, though, for in time (a long time), he knocked me into some sort of singing shape. But being totally unmusical and tone deaf, I was one he could not forget. I thank God for the discipline of the choral life and for the great hymns of the Church that burned into my young mind.

And for the weddings. Instead of the usual shilling (five pence) we got for choir practice, midweek evensong and two Sunday services, we were given a bonus of two shillings and sixpence – a whole half a crown – for a Saturday wedding. With a number of RAF bases around

North Wiltshire at that time, we did quite well. The young pilots (though they looked old to me) would arrive in their convertible Aston Martins, the cars decked with white garlands, the men with Brylcreem and swell moustaches! Very often the best man would be in RAF uniform too, and I remember one big, tall fellow with the biggest handle-bar moustache I had ever seen. It covered the whole front of his nose. I was so taken by it that I stopped singing and just stared, fascinated. He gave me a brimming smile and a big wink. . .which helped offset the telling-off I got from the choirmaster afterwards.

I often got such smiles from wedding parties, and perhaps they thought that the dark-haired, brown-eyed, rosy-cheeked youngster looked angelic, what with his black smock and white ruffle collar. Nothing could have been less true. They should have seen us afterwards in the graveyard outside, or on dark nights when we went early to choir practice in order to ambush unsuspecting choristers as they arrived.

It was these antics in the churchyard which brought my choir years to an end. Some older boys began to go too far, and the innocent fun turned into bullying. There was a punch-up behind the graves when my brother went in at the deep end to defend me, and some real 'roughing up' as warfare developed between two rival groups of choirboys. My father got to hear about it, and one dark night he hid behind a tree nearby. When the bully boys began their capers, he jumped out and off they ran, startled at being caught in the act. The choirmaster was puzzled by a number of absentees that night.

My father withdrew us from the choir for a while over this 'ill discipline', much to Mother's disappointment. Shortly afterwards, we left to live in Southbourne, Bournemouth, and Mother made sure that we joined the Sunday School and attended church without fail. But there was no more choir.

Those days in Bournemouth at the end of the war

seem to belong to a different age. I remember playing hopscotch in the street; a party on the green to celebrate the end of the war, with my first taste of jelly and ice-cream (an unknown luxury during the war); the soldiers coming home, some of them for the first time since the fighting began; a great bonfire in the street on which we burnt effigies of 'Old Hitler and Mussolini'. . . . It seemed as if a dark and evil time had come to an end, and there was new hope in the world. The British Empire still stood and we were proud of the pink which covered two-thirds of the map on the wall. As our old school teacher told us, it was to be 'handed on to you ungrateful twerps!'

I remember the bold prayers of the schoolmaster in regular morning assembly: 'Defend this great Empire. . . defeat its enemies. . .build a land fit for heroes. . . .' They seemed long prayers, but they gripped us with wonder and even fear. We learned through them a respect for the Almighty and for all human life, and a pride in our nation. What a difference to the humanist bunch who have taken over today in many of our schools, with permissive sex education, watered down, non-religious assemblies, and even discussions about fitting condom machines in schools. How *ridiculous*. Darkness and demons have invaded many education authorities today.

During that time in Bournemouth I grew to love Fishermen's Walk, the Chines, walking on the shingle on Beachy Head while Father worked as an engineer, first at Hurn airport and later, after the war, building the famous 'Brabazon' aeroplane. When I returned in 1980 for my great Bournemouth Tent Crusade, more than one thousand were converted and we saw two new churches planted in the town. It was a joy to meet people who had lived in the same street back in 1946 – and lead them to Jesus. When I told my mother about it, tears came to her eyes at the way God was honouring the vow she had made all those years ago.

17

3 A Bus Trip to Heaven

Salvation is the golden string
God winds up till it comes to an end in heaven
                                    – William Blake

One of the most frequent questions I get asked by journalists around the world is: 'How did you find God?' What is conversion?

It is not what most people think it is: a splash with water, a submerging under water, a confirmation, a confession, agreeing a doctrine, becoming a church member, joining a group or sect... None of these has anything to do with our personal salvation.

Instead, conversion is a new birth, a new beginning, a crisis, an exodus, a regeneration, a transformation into a new life.

One of the hallmarks is certainty. We pass from death, dreariness and boredom to life, joy and assurance. For me, this meant being absolutely sure that I was accepted by the Father: my old life blotted out, the dark shadow across my conscience lifted. William Percy has written a simple rhyme which sums up this simple truth:

> I heard a bird at break of day
> Sing from the autumn trees
> A song so mystical and calm,
> So full of certainties.
> No man, I think, could listen long
> Except upon his knees.
> Yet this was but a simple bird
> Alone, among the trees.

Back in Chippenham after the war, Father came home from the factory one evening and told us in passing that he had seen a poster about a film show. It was free, with a free bus trip to Bristol thrown in.

I could hardly believe it. 'Are you sure, Dad?'

'Well, I think it said free of charge. That's what made me take a second look.'

'Do have another peep at it, then, Dad, and let me know the details.'

A couple of days later, I had forgotten all about it. Dad and I were chatting over tea.

'By the way, I saw the poster again on the factory notice board. It's this Saturday. You have to get the bus at six o'clock at the corner of London Road by the post office. And it is free.'

I looked up eagerly from my chips and egg, and declared (with my mouth full), 'Oh, I'm going then'.

I loved Humphrey Bogart, John Wayne, Jane Russell, Cary Grant, Doris Day. . . . But it cost one shilling and ninepence to get into the Gaumont in Chippenham, so this was fantastic. *And* a free trip to Bristol, twenty-five miles away.

As my father got up from the table, tidying away his plate so he could head off into the garden, he added:

'By the way, it sounds like something religious.'

Suddenly a dark cloud appeared overhead. No wonder it was free, then.

But it was something different, and I had said I was going. So that Saturday evening, 6 April 1955, there I was, standing by the little post office in London Road. The bus came, the door opened and I climbed in. The first person I saw as I mounted the steps was Mr Balch, one of my former Sunday School teachers. He had taught me three or four years before, and ever since then had been asking Mother why I was missing from church. Little did he know that whenever I saw him I would dive down

19

a back lane or double back up the street and go home the long way round.

'Hello, Melvin. Nice to see you', he smiled in greeting.

I went and sat down at the back of the bus, which was two-thirds full – mostly with old ladies, I noticed.

We were in Bristol by ten to seven, and I got out of the bus as quickly as I could and made my way into the cinema. I got a seat down on the left, about five rows from the front. One thing which struck me was the noise. In those days you could be ordered out for being noisy or raucous; but here people were chatting out loud and everyone seemed friendly. A sailor and his blonde girlfriend pushed by to sit a few seats away to my left. I was comforted by the sight of his blue and white bib and flat sailor's hat, and decided it couldn't be too bad here, since sailors were not generally too religious.

The film began. It was a Billy Graham film. It featured four different people: one a film star, one a businessman and two others, all of whom had lives filled with problems and distress and heartaches. Each went independently to a meeting led by Billy Graham (then quite young), and one by one they were converted to a life following Jesus. I did not feel it had much to do with me, since they all lived on a much higher plane (though I noticed they still had troubles).

So I sat there, not involved in the film at all, until it ended with a five- or ten-minute sermon from Billy Graham. And then I was gripped. I was gripped by what he had to say, gripped by the Bible message, gripped by the powerful Word of God. I felt an overwhelming sense that I was a sinner, that I was not living rightly, that I owed everything to God, that I had broken His laws and was in danger of being lost in Hell one day and, almost as bad, of missing the best in life which God had planned for me.

Then the film ended, the lights came on, and a short, tubby vicar walked onto the stage, his neck bursting over a tight dog collar. He was no evangelist. But he was gentle, and he asked folk to come down to the front of the cinema, to pray together and confess Jesus. I was not sure what he meant, but I knew he was calling us to stand up and dedicate ourselves to Jesus and start living the sort of life called for in the film.

By this time I had my head down below the seat in front, and my mind was in a turmoil. If I went out there, I told myself, it had to be everything. I wanted no hypocrisy, no half-measures, no giving it a try. God had to mean everything, or He meant nothing. People seemed to be going forward from all over the cinema, and somebody pushed along the row to get past me. I looked up and saw the sailor, and behind him the blonde. I sat up again, but still struggling. It would mean everything. Could I keep it up? Surely I would fail? All these doubts and questions crowded into my mind. But finally I realized I had no choice. I had to go. I was shaking – I felt such awe, such a conviction, such brokenness, such a fear of God, that I could not do anything else.

I stood up and soon found myself at the front. I was led to the second row on the right and there a white-haired old man read some scriptures of the Bible to me and talked to me. Afterwards, I didn't remember anything he said, for I was so full of joy, almost ecstasy, as if I was having a jaccuzzi bath inside! I was washed clean, but by a heavenly power. Everything seemed new, white, fresh, wholesome.

I went out walking on air, with a hearty handshake from the old man and the vicar with the double chin. I was the last one out, so I expected to have to walk home. But there was one bus still sitting in the deserted market square and it was mine. Mr Balch saw me coming and opened the door and I clambered on, red-faced and embarrassed, since everyone was looking at me. The front seat was empty this time, so I jumped into it and the bus revved up and set off down the A420 for Chippenham and home.

That night a seventeen-year-old had taken a coach trip to a far greater place – Heaven. Little did I realize then where else that decision was going to take me over the next thirty-five years, proclaiming the Gospel to millions and leading tens of thousands out of despair into a new life of hope and peace and health with Jesus. Perhaps if I had known the demands and hardship of such a calling, I might have got off the bus a little earlier! But on that bus journey I was busy just trying to understand what had happened, distracted a little by the whispers that floated to me from behind: 'He's done it then?' What had I done wrong now, I wondered. 'He's got it then?' Had I caught some disease? 'Wonder if it'll last?' Did God's blessings wear out? 'He's one of us now.' Was this some kind of special club? 'Wonder if he'll join the choir?' No more punch-ups in the graveyard again? 'Hope he's in church on Sunday.' Well, I wanted to be, so why not? The voices died away.

All I knew was that I was born again. I did not know all the jargon or the theology or the tradition or any of the other things I had to learn (and unlearn, later). But I knew that I had come alive that day.

The story goes of a Roman soldier who sent to Caesar asking for permission to commit suicide. He was miserable and dispirited and wanted to kill himself. Caesar looked at him: 'Man,' he said, 'were you ever really *alive*?' Jesus said: 'I am come that they might have life and that they might have it more abundantly.'

4 Heading for the River Without a Bridge

Sure of God's guiding hand, we never lose the certainty
                                    Dietrich Bonhoeffer

Looking back now, I recognize the vital elements that took place the memorable night I was converted. But first a word about conversion itself. Many people ask me what 'conversion' means. It is hard to explain, for they are in darkness and 'the natural man understandeth not the things of the Spirit of God'. It was once said: 'You can no more tell what you don't have, than you can come back from where you haven't been.' And yet Jesus said: 'Unless you are converted. . .you will by no means enter the Kingdom of Heaven.'

The word 'conversion' is made up of two Latin words: **con** meaning 'with' and **vertare** meaning 'to turn'. **Conversion**, then, is a turning to a new direction. At conversion, you pass from the kingdom of self-interest into the kingdom of God and His interests. There is literally a world of difference between heaven and hell, and at conversion you change worlds. But it is not just a turning, it is a turning *with*. In this new world, you and God work out life – together. You supply the willingness; He supplies the power. You commit yourself to Him; He commits Himself to you. The lonely, struggling, orphan life is gone. You have a new father and He has a new child.

So it was in my case. As a young man I was restless and unhappy. I found no pleasure in the world and certainly no pleasure in the church. Then I sat in a service where someone presented the Gospel in a way I had never heard before. That night I was radically converted. God's hand reached down from heaven and lifted me from the kingdom of self into the kingdom of God. What was it like?

First, I felt my guilt.

People want to remain in their old ways, habits and sins. In one British city, a new market was built which was clean and sanitary. But the people who ran the stalls in the dirty old market would not move into the new one because, as one put it, 'the new market is so clean it is just like a hospital. It makes us feel sick.' In the same way we cling to our old life of apathy, staleness, pride, arrogance and selfishness. As the hymnwriter put it:

> He took the suffering human race
> He made each wound, each weakness clear –
> And struck his finger on the place
> And said, 'Thou ailest here, and here'.

God strikes us only to heal. Guilt hurts, but it is really God's love at work within us. It pushes us towards God to seek release and freedom. And not just us, but many people in this dark hour of history. All over the world, people are realizing that Jesus is just what they need. Someone has suggested that each letter in his name can sum this up, JESUS: Jesus Exactly Suits Us Sinners!

Second, I felt humbled and sorry.

God wants us to stop resisting Him, to surrender. 'For the Lord takes pleasure in his people; he adorns the humble with victory' (Psalm 149, verse 4). A prison chaplain who had been a professional wrestler would tell the prisoners: 'I could get out of any hold my opponent put on me.' Then he would pause, and add: 'All I had to do was give in and the referee would break the hold!' The chaplain would go on to say that the answer lay not in trying but in trusting; not in wrestling but in resting; not in striving but in surrender. He added: 'It's not easy to admit you can't do it alone. But you must let Christ take hold!'

It was very humbling to have to admit that I could not manage on my own. It was very hard to say sorry to God for the mess I had made of things. God has no time for quick, easy apologies like Toad's in *The Wind in the Willows*: Toad is so bad that he ends up being lectured to by the overbearing Badger in the smoking room of Toad Hall, and finally gives in and repents. But later, when asked by the other animals, 'Did you, did you repent as Badger said?' Toad replies, red-faced, 'I only did it to please him and am still the same as before.' But for me it was real repentance, bringing forth real tears and with a real change of heart, a real breaking of my spirit. I broke. I was God's. I was at his feet. He conquered me. I was overcome, smashed, broken into little pieces. I wanted to obey *Him*. Kneeling at the foot of the cross, I was lifted to the dazzling heights of splendour.

Thirdly, I began to feel a great love for Jesus.
A famous Rabbi, Rabbi Duncan, tells how a woman came to him one day complaining of coldness of heart. She said she did not love the Lord any more. The Rabbi looked her full in the face and asked: 'How much would you take to give him up?' She considered his question for a moment and then, realizing how much God meant to her, she felt a sudden rush of emotion, and burst out: 'Oh, I would not give Him up for all the world!'

That is the measure of the love we are given, even if at times we do not feel it. I have held on to that simple love, no matter how many around me have fallen to the right or to the left, no matter how many have doubted or given up. I fell in love with Jesus that night thirty six years ago. It is one of the chief things which has preserved my faith through those years: I have kept in love with Jesus. Indeed, I love Him more and more.

It is a good check of your relationship with Jesus, to look and see how simple, sincere, genuine and pure your love for Jesus is today. Have you slipped into being a critical, know-it-all, demanding sort of lover? Or are you a gentle, peaceable, sweet and trusting lover? Stay in love with Jesus!

Fourthly, peace reigned within me from that hour.
As I alighted from the bus at 11 o'clock that Saturday night in 1955 and walked down the quiet lanes of Chippenham to the little cottage in Wood Lane where I lived, I glowed with peace. I had been uncertain when I walked into that cinema. But since that day I have never been unsure or lacked God's peace.

It was this peace that I wanted to share with others. And it was this peace which gave me the courage to do so. When I testified the next day and the following weeks, and told the men on the building sites, they laughed and mocked. Some even cursed and swore and made me the butt of their jokes, leaving me on the top of the scaffolding at the end of the day without a ladder; or filling my wellingtons with cement; or pinching my sandwich box; or leaving me stranded on the site. One tough brickie said, 'I'll give you three months. . . .'

It's been a long three months! When I met the man again after a number of years, he admitted, 'Yes, I was wrong, you are one of those who kept going.'

It is said Gladstone loved the text 'The peace of God which passeth all understanding keep your hearts and minds in the knowledge and love of God.' If your own mind is filled with fear, defeat and turmoil, then practise thinking about God for as many minutes of the day as you can. I have learnt to concentrate on the Lord and rest in his peace.

26

In Colossians it says: 'Christ made peace by the blood of His cross'. Again: 'the chastisement of our peace was upon Him'. On the Cross, through the propitiation, the one and only substitute Christ – I was now free, and at tranquillity and peace for ever. It was for me He had died, I was now redeemed for ever through His marvellous Grace. Everything depended on what Christ had done on that Cross. It was not the symbol of the Cross; it was more than that. As Eric Dando put it—

A Cross without a Christ is a ritualism
A Christ without a Cross is a rationalism
but a Christ on a cross is a redemption.

My peace was from His Sacrifice, Jesus said:

'That in ME YE MIGHT HAVE PEACE. . .'
(John. 16:33)

Fifthly, I overflowed with thankfulness.
One of the Marx Brothers and his wife adopted three children. Every night he would tell the first child how they had always wanted a son, and they had looked at hundreds of wee boys, and had travelled many miles until one day they at last found the boy who was *their* boy. Then he would continue the 'great story' of how they wanted a girl too: they had looked at hundreds of wee girls, and had travelled many miles until they found *her*. By this time, the third adopted child would be bubbling with excitement about this story, of which she was so much a part. She would pull her daddy's hand with her chubby fingers until he came to include her in the 'great story'. The writer told how, for twenty years, his children would not go to bed without the 'great story' being told. One day, as he was mowing the lawn, his son approached him, saying 'Dad, may I talk to you about the "great story"?'

27

As the elderly comedian followed his son into the study, he wondered if perhaps he had done the right thing in telling them the story of their adoption. He waited apprehensively as his son shut the door and turned to face him.

'Dad, the girls have asked me to speak to you on their behalf and to say this: *Thank you, Dad, for taking us in.*'

How thankful you and I ought to be that we have been adopted into the great family of God. We too should say, 'Thank you, Father, for taking us in.'

Finally, I felt sure God had accepted me.

This assurance is one of Christ's greatest gifts, and I got it that night and have never lost it. When I finished my prayer of faith in the cinema, the old man leading me asked, gently and quietly:

'Do you know you're saved?'

And I was able to say with the most positive certainty:

'Yes!' Oh, yes, I knew and still know that I am saved by God's grace alone.

In *The Wind in the Willows*, Badger tells Rat and Mole that, for the wayward Toad, 'The hour has come. . . He will be the most converted animal there ever was.' Well, that's how I felt that night: converted; God's animal through and through. It was a sudden, instant, miraculous change.

Soon afterwards, of course, the devil was telling me, 'There's nothing in it. It won't last.' And he recruited my work-mates on the building site, the carpenters, brickies, electricians, plasterers and plumbers: 'There's nothing in it. It won't last.' But I soon learnt – and have told a million people since – *The devil never tells lost people they are not saved. He only tells saved people they are not saved.*

God spoke to me that night in the cinema and gave me the assurance that He would always be with me.

'Live in me and let me live in you' says Jesus in John's gospel (Chapter 15, verse 4). He gave me courage with the certainty, which enabled me to stand up before my friends at work, and before strangers in the open air in my home town of Chippenham.

You can look like a Christian and act like one; you can sing all the hymns and show signs of Christianity in your works. But it means nothing if you have not met Jesus, if you have not touched Him. I knew Him that night and touched Him, and He has never left me.

Jesus said: 'He that believeth in me, tho' he were dead, yet shall he live. . .whoever believeth in me shall never die.' In John Bunyan's book, *Pilgrim's Progress*, a character called Mr Feeblemind speaks about his longing for heaven. He cannot comprehend heaven with his mind. But he says:

'I am resolved to run when I can, to go when I cannot run, to creep when I am not strong enough to go. . .my mind is beyond the river that hath no bridge.'

Is your mind, your heart, resolved to get 'beyond the river that hath no bridge'? Have you this magnificent assurance of positive certainty?

5 Hellfire in the Cotswolds

The great end of life is not knowledge but action
                                            Thomas Huxley

*The urgency of the Gospel is impossible to
exaggerate*

                                            Reinhardt Bonnke

Following my conversion in the cinema in Bristol, I threw myself enthusiastically into service for Jesus. I went along to the local Salvation Army citadel on the 'bridge' over the River Avon, in the centre of Chippenham. It was here Mother had sent me to Sunday School, or Bible class, after the punch-ups outside the Church of England church. So it was natural for me to go back to 'train' with such a strong evangelistic force.

I enjoyed the openair meetings, and started preaching – first with little one-minute gospel talks, then later with four-minute testimonies (telling the story of my conversion) at every street corner in the town. I joined the band, playing 'not very well at all' but receiving great patience from Bandmaster Tinson, who was himself an outstanding musician.

Then one day, old Brother Cox (an ex-officer) asked me to accompany him on a preaching engagement to a small chapel congregation in the countryside, adding that he would like me to give a short testimony. This was the start of regular trips out to preach to small congregations scattered in rural areas in the heart of the beautiful Cotswolds. A little later he asked me to preach my first sermon.

'I will lead the service and give the main sermon', he told me. 'You give a short sermon early in the meeting. Keep it short and weave in plenty of scripture.'

Thus Castle Coombe, England's prettiest village, was on the receiving end of my first gospel sermon. Twelve people were given eight minutes of hellfire, a red-hot, punchy, straight message about Christ, His cross and His resurrection, His power to save. I even made an appeal for sinners to come to Jesus. No one responded. I was disappointed, but afterwards dear Alfred Cox put his hand on my shoulder and said, 'We have to sow the seed, my boy. One day God will give us a harvest.'

My next sermon was in the Salvation Army Sunday-night gospel meeting in Cirencester, Gloucestershire, again with Alfred. This time thirty people attended. On this occasion I spoke for twelve minutes, again appealed, but again no one came forward. Afterwards, Alfred comforted me once more, 'Do not be discouraged. Keep on sowing the seed. For the Bible says, bread cast upon the waters will not return void.' I wondered when it would start! But God was patient, even if I was not.

Some of the old preachers – Mr Whale, Mr Smith, and others I mixed with – were patient with me. The old Wiltshire preachers were nicknamed in those days 'the slaughter-house preachers' because they spoke so often and so much about the blood of Jesus, about Christ becoming the one 'led as a sheep to the slaughter'. I loved the preaching of the shed blood. It has never left me. All those men – now almost all gone to their reward – were very severe and strict, and their humour, if they had any, was very dry. They kept a close eye on 'the young preacher Banks'. I had to toe the line, speak when spoken to, not go over time in my sermons, not worry if there was no immediate result.

And I had to report promptly at the Salvation Army hall each Wednesday for Bible fellowship; and at seven o'clock each Sunday morning for 'knee drill' – the prayer meeting. If I was late, or failed to turn up, I was deemed not fit to preach or take part in a public service, and had a kindly but firm ticking-off. I did not always appreciate the discipline of that period, but now, looking back, I love and respect the background it gave me. For one thing, I was never allowed to get bigheaded.

Old Bud Robinson was a Nazarene preacher, eccentric, powerful, unlearned but radiant in holiness, a brilliant preacher who led many to Christ. After a sermon someone would say, 'That was a marvellous message, best I ever heard. . . .' Then the old man would pray quickly to the Lord – 'Don't let me get puffed up. . . .' Then someone would come along and say, 'Uncle Buddy,' (that's what they called him) 'that was the worst preaching I ever heard . . . .' Then the old man would pray 'Lord, don't let me get puffed down!'

But God gifts even untalented people, and these old fellows saw this no doubt, and that gave me confidence, and a stern type of love. They frowned at over-emotionalism, but sought to draw out a real gift they evidently saw that 'young Banks' had from the Lord.

I remember the story of the little boy who was honoured by going round Buckingham Palace in London with a special school party – it was a rare visit, not very often allowed around the Royal residence. He saw luscious grapes in a greenhouse, and asked a tall man nearby if he could buy some? The man replied, 'No, but I will give you some free'. Later the gardener came along, sought the boy out and gave him a big bunch of juicy, bright, ripe grapes. The gardener said to the lad, 'The King sent these along for you, you asked him for some, he never sells his grapes'. *The king always gives them freely*. . . Yes, King Jesus gives his gifts FREELY, to whom He will. The 'wind bloweth where it listeth and we only hear the sound thereof'.

So those early days were so important with those old Wiltshire preachers. They made me realize that God had given, *me freely of his gifts*, that I must seek after my calling, I must prepare for it and in it. Among many lessons I learned the truths they emphasized still live in my heart. I am glad I made a note of some of them on an old writing pad; here are a few I jotted down:

'Christianity on impulse is not discipleship'

'God isn't going to stampede us into the Kingdom'

'Some get saved quickly on enthusiasm, but backslide on principle'!

One famous prayer of theirs I remember went like this – 'O God, work through me what you have worked into me. . .'! The daring, of standing in openair meetings, with friends of mine from school-days walking by, watching me singing and preaching, very often calling out, 'Hey Melvin, are you in the Sally Army all gone barmy then?' or just laughing and giggling as they went by – it was a real challenge and trial, and gave me a lot of courage for even more daring escapades later.

My enthusiasm had an unfortunate effect on the Major who interviewed me for the Salvation Army Bible College. At about the age of eighteen I felt that I could do with some more training. The more enthusiastic I became, the more dejected the Major got, since I lacked a lot of the Bible knowledge that should go with it. He asked me what was 'the love chapter in the Bible'. I could not answer (it is, of course, 1 Corinthians chapter 13).

'You need a lot of teaching', he concluded, with an anxious sigh, but I was accepted for training as a Salvation Army officer.

So in August 1958 I turned up at the famous William Booth training centre in Camberwell, then run by a radiant, spiritual Dane called Commissioner Karl Westergaard. I was an innocent country boy, but the Salvation Army's evangelistic and social training was very thorough, and I was soon introduced to the not-so-innocent world that lay around me.

I was soon tramping through Soho, London, speaking for Christ to lost men in the striptease dens, witnessing to the first homosexuals I had ever met, I had never heard of men going round dressing and talking like women, so I stared with unbelief at such people and their antics! I knelt and prayed and gave tea and food to men under arches in the dark Stepney area of the East End, men who slept out all night in the cold, homeless with no bed, but their 'sheets of newspapers' covering them. I spoke to prostitutes and tried to show them the error of their ways. One attempted to hit me when I suggested she 'start a new moral life' on the edge of Piccadilly, centre of Manchester. I preached in men's social centres to hundreds of alcoholics and poverty-struck, sad, dejected men in prisons, on the 'skid rows' of the big cities. It was an eye-opener revealing the deep sin and abject despair of the lowest of humanity. The Salvation Army training is the finest in the world in regard to man's social needs. I am glad I went through such a course. I still deeply respect it.

There was of course more to it than this side: theological studies, English (even my spelling improved a lot!), Bible studies, how to do church accounts, or run a corps (church), or preach (although I was regarded to be so poor I was only ever given one chance to preach, then not given another!), how to counsel people, and many behind-the-scenes preparations for being a church leader.

The nine months spent at William Booth College were among the most memorable of my life, and I am still being shaped by them. Shortly afterwards, I felt God calling me out of the Salvation Army, and I eventually found 'the house of my pilgrimage' in the charismatic renewal movement. But God's kingdom is bigger than any one type of church. The Army might have lost an officer, but they have never lost a friend.

I learned early to face discouragements. I remember preaching to a small congregation in one place as a teenage preacher. One old lady said within my hearing, 'I didn't think much of him, I don't think he'll ever come to anything, he'll not last very long.' My lip trembled, a tear came to my eye, for a moment I thought, 'Will I ever make it?' For a few days afterwards, thinking of the lady's words, I was somewhat discouraged but spent extra time reading the Holy Scriptures. I remembered what the early preachers had told me – 'Always drive the devil away with the Word of God!' I overcame it after a week or so, and pressed on.

Years later I was in that area preaching at a huge, crammed rally in the public auditorium of the town, hundreds were saved, many marvellously healed. This lady had died by now but her daughter came to the meeting. She asked me if I recognised her and with a few reminiscences reminded me of her mother. I smiled and said courteously I remembered her Mum all right! She then announced loudly that her mother – 'Always did like your preaching and said you would go a long way and have a great ministry. . .' Well you can't win, can you?

I certainly have learned not to take seriously most things I hear in this way or at least to treat them very lightly!

My greatest encouragement, even during these early years, came not from what people said to me, but from what God enabled me to do. Sometimes He would allow me a glimpse of the 'miraculous' ministry that lay ahead.

For example: one day, a few years later on, when I was based in Newcastle-upon-Tyne, I was walking home from work, very tired and hungry. It was about six o'clock, and I wanted to get home so that I could grab something to eat before hurrying out to meet some new converts. I was about to take my usual short cut, when I suddenly felt an urge to go the long way round. How ridiculous, I thought to myself as I set off; why am going all the way round here?

Then, as I turned another corner, I ran straight into Dolly, a little old lady whom I knew. I had spoken to her a number of times at her front door, when out canvassing to get people along to our church. But now she looked distressed; she avoided my eyes and, with a mumbled greeting, passed quickly by me. She was a few yards down the road when I realized that something was drastically wrong.

'Hey, Dolly', I called, and ran to catch up with her. 'Come here. There's something troubling you.' She backed away and stood against the wall of a house.

'I'm going to do away with myself! I'm heading for the Tyne [the river]. I'm fed up, no one cares, I'm so sad and sick with life, Melvin', she cried.

I let her cry for some minutes and she spilled out all her troubles: her son never went to see her, she was alone, no one cared, she was desperately lonely. . .so it went on. I was soon chatting away with her, telling her I was going to come and see her later that night, bring her some books, have a cup of tea with her, come and fetch her and take her to church, take her home again, help get supper ready, even contact her so if she wanted. Within ten or fifteen minutes she had brightened up.

'No need for any foolish talk about the Tyne', I said. 'It's too cold to jump in tonight, anyway; wait till Summer and the warmer weather.' Dolly was soon laughing uncontrollably, and I escorted her back to her door. I said a quick prayer, and over the next few days did all I said I would. She later told me it had been no idle threat: ten minutes later and she would have thrown herself in the river, had she not bumped into me. The last I saw of her was a few years ago: she was still going to church in Newcastle – happy, bright and full of hope in her old age.

Back in Chippenham, what most characterized me was my enthusiasm. I was gripped by enthusiasm and wanted to share the message about Jesus with all and sundry as never before. How enthusiastically do we do God's job?

Several years later, when a young evangelist, I was invited to speak to a Christian Union at a college not too far away from where I live. I had received no clear directions and the only instruction was a request to be at the college at 4.30 p.m., and an indication that the meeting would be held in a room off the main corridor.

I arrived at the meeting early and waited in the entrance hall, expecting to be met by a member of the Christian Union. After kicking my heels and reading endless notices advertising student activities, I decided to find where the Union met. I proceeded along what I assumed was the main corridor and peeked into the rooms. It was an old college, and all the heavy oak doors had 'spy holes' which were covered by brass plates. They could be moved to enable a passing lecturer to look into the rooms without disrupting classes.

The first room accommodated a dozen students, some with their feet on the desks, and they were obviously relaxing and apparently having a good time together. I didn't sense that they were waiting for a speaker!

The second room had about nine students, who were huddled around a couple of desks which were pushed together, and they were engrossed in a card game in which a portion of their student grants was being passed round the table. Again, I sensed this was not my flock!

On looking into a third room my heart sank. A dozen people, all sitting bolt upright in their seats, facing the front, dressed immaculately and all looking as if they had lost five pounds and found fifty. Yes, you've guessed it – I had found the Christian Union! What is missing in

37

Britain, and which I've discovered on my travels is so evident in Christ's body around the world? One vital, urgent quality and virtue has been lost in the UK – PASSION! *Where is the passion of heart* that is missing so much today? George Fox inspired his followers with the cry – 'Go and tell them about the Lamb of God, till you can tell them no more'.

I was borne along in those early days by the supreme wonder of the Gospel. I am inspired today more than ever by that same Gospel, that same Divine book: the Bible, that same Christ of Calvary, that same Holy Spirit – *that same passion drives me on*!

> Society is dreadfully sick
> the opportunity is vast
> the harvest is ready
> the world gasps for Christ!

It is time for the Kingdom of light to penetrate the kingdom of darkness. The blood of perishing millions is in my hands and yours!

JOIN ME – in eating, drinking, breathing, living, *loving and shouting this message*, with joy and burning, blazing intensity and enthusiasm *till our dying day*!

6 *The Drunken Preacher*

We few, we happy few, we band of brothers. . .
William Shakespeare: Henry V

Having left the Salvation Army, I ended up in the early
1960s at the Bethshan Church in Newcastle-upon-Tyne.
I had been attending for about six months when people
started urging me to seek the filling of the Holy Spirit.
They had by this time become friends, so I took them
seriously. But I nevertheless insisted that I had always
had the Holy Spirit. Hadn't I been born again? There
was little argument or theological debate. These keen
young Christians just kept opening their Bibles to show
me how, for example, all the disciples had their names
written in the 'lamb's book of life' and yet still needed
to wait at Jerusalem to be 'endued with power'; or how
the new believers at Cornelius' house, according to Peter,
'received like we did at the beginning'. I held stubbornly
to the views learnt during my evangelical upbringing,
which at that time largely denied any need for a 'second
blessing' or for the gift of tongues.

But there was a hunger inside me. What was all this
joy, exuberance, enthusiasm, dedication and power of
these young pentecostal Christians? I began to think
more, study more, pray more. I discovered in the
Bible that joy came from the Holy Spirit: the early
believers 'were filled with joy and with the Holy
Ghost'. I discovered, too, that power was also part
of the experience: Jesus told His followers, 'Ye shall
receive power after the Holy Ghost is come upon you'.
Yet I felt so powerless.

The Church seemed powerless, too, Satan was on the loose, destroying young people – even children – with devil worship, witchcraft, occult games and books. All around was bloodshed, fear, hatred and moral degradation. It seemed to me that we needed more than ever what the apostles had. The original Gospel was impossible without the original power.

But did we need to speak in tongues? And did they need to be brash, loud, exuberant? Could I not receive a blessing without tongues? After all, had I not read that Kathryn Khulman called the Holy Spirit a gentleman? Later, when asked if she spoke with tongues, she replied: 'I was filled with love when He came to me.' Only later still did she admit, with some reluctance, that she did speak with tongues. Was I on the wrong track? Thoughts crowded into my mind from every direction. Still not convinced about all the details, I came to realize that my life was sadly lacking. I began to pray: 'O Holy Spirit, come!'

It was on a Saturday night in October 1962. That night at the Bethshan we had a visiting pentecostal preacher from London, Pastor Harold Young. The church was filled, the teaching on the Holy Spirit was superb, and as the meeting ended, Pastor Young invited seekers after the fullness of the Holy Spirit to come into the side room for the laying on of hands and a time of receiving.

This was not for me, and soon I was one hundred yards down the road with my wife, Lilian, heading for a bus-stop and the bus which would take us the five miles to Blaydon, where we then lived. Suddenly I stopped, and declared to my wife with dismay:

'I have forgotten the crayons and pencils for the children for tomorrow's Sunday School.'

'Do you need them?'

'Yes; there is something I must prepare for the kiddies tomorrow.' So saying, I dashed back to the church and opened the door into the side room. But I heard voices, and realized that this was the group of seekers. I stood half in, half out of the door, looking around for the crayons.

Suddenly, the tall, dignified preacher from London looked up from the circle of people in front of him, and looked at me.

'Young man, do you want God's power?'

At his voice, I stopped in my tracks. I did not know what to say. My hand had almost reached the pencils. The voice thundered again:

'Do you?'

I could hardly say 'No, I don't want the power of the Holy Spirit in all its fullness. I just want the pencils.' Besides, I *did* want God's power. I still had all my reservations about speaking in tongues and so on, but somehow I blurted out, 'Well, yes, I do, but. . .'

'Come on, then, down here!' He pointed to an empty seat.

I made my way forward nervously and sat down. And my mind was suddenly flooded with all the things I had read about the Holy Spirit in previous months, and I was filled with all my desire and hunger for more of the living God.

Soon, large, warm hands were laid on my head and a voice, Pastor Young's, rang out: 'Receive the Holy Ghost in Jesus' name.' I just thought of how much I loved the Lord, how devoted I was to Him, how I wanted to do His will, walk in His ways, obtain His blessing. 'Receive. . .receive. . .in the lovely name of Jesus. . .in the name of Jesus. . .' I remember the soft voice whispering.

Then came such a gushing, such a warm wave over my whole being, such love flooded me, drenched me, evaporated me; such a sense of glory, light, joy. I spoke, I just wanted to use my tongue and magnify the Saviour. And as I used my tongue, I spoke in another language. No one taught me any words; I never heard anyone

41

speak around me. I was lost in Jesus, and this tongue began. All I was conscious of was speaking beautiful words of power, in a language I had not known before. Indeed, the only language I have ever learnt is English. But this was so beautiful. I just wanted to speak it for ever.

Indeed, half-an-hour must have passed before I came-to fully. I still felt heady, and wanted to share my experience with everybody. I felt like someone who was drunk, but not with poisonous alcohol; I was light with divine ecstasy. I felt a fire had burned through me. Pastor Young put his arm round me. He had seen thousands filled with the Holy Spirit, but he still loved to see people charged with the divine dynamite; still loved to see 'fire fall'. His eyes shone with love and joy, radiated on his long, slim face, and he told me: 'Keep speaking in tongues, my boy. Every day, praise the Lord with audible words, and in the Spirit, and in tongues. *Keep full of the power.*'

My wife had become very impatient by the time I staggered – literally – out of the church door. After all, 35 – 40 minutes to pick up a few crayons and pencils was a little hard to understand, and when she saw me stumbling towards her, she was aghast!

'Lord Jesus, wonderful Jesus, Jesus, Jesus, I love you. . .' I was saying in a loving, adoring voice. People passing by stared, some amused, some unbelieving, at the sight of this 'drunken' preacher. We moved off, me leaning on Lilian; and she could hear people discussing me:

'Is he mad?'

'No, he's just drunk.'

My wife helped me onto the bus which would take us home, and the conductor smiled at her:

'He's had a good fill up tonight!'

'He certainly has', Lilian replied.

'Must be some powerful stuff.'

'Yes, it's the strongest on earth.'

'Must be an old vintage.'

'Two thousand years old, in fact.'

'No wonder it's knocked him out, then.'

'I doubt if he'll ever be the same again.'

'What do you call that wine?'

'It's the new wine, a heavenly variety.'

'It looks as if it was out of this world.'

Lilian went on to explain to the conductor about the power of the Holy Spirit coming upon me. The conductor just scratched his head:

'I didn't think religion could do something as good as this for anyone.'

For days afterwards I felt an inner power, a joy, a sweetness. But I soon learned I could not live on one day's experience, so I fuelled myself with prayer. I found myself seeking longer times of prayer, so I could wait on the Lord, praise Him, tell Him how much I loved Him, and to speak long and often in the new tongues He had given me. And when I witnessed, I felt a stronger conviction, a stronger urge to persuade them and convince them; and also that a new fruitfulness was about to begin. But I had to learn over many years how to abide in the Holy Spirit and keep in the fullness, the gifts, the fruits the anointings and the powers of the Holy Spirit.

This is some of what I learned about how to 'keep full of the power', as the old pentecostal preacher had entreated.

1 Heed the command

The command of God's word, 'Be filled with the Spirit', is not to be treated lightly, for it may spell the difference between a fruitful life and a fruitless one, a life of spiritual power or spiritual defeat. Some may criticize, or endeavour to complicate the simple command, but there are no grounds for rejecting the truth of the Scriptures. The Word of God and not the opinion of men will be our final judge. Jesus's purpose in coming from the glories of heaven to our world of sin was to save the lost, and to destroy the works of the devil. As Jesus carried out His ministry in the power of the Holy Spirit, so is it His purpose that we carry His work in the power of that same Spirit.

2 Keep a need of the Holy Spirit

The sinner will never turn to Christ until he realizes his need of a Saviour. In the same way, a believer will never accept Christ as his baptizer until he realizes how much he needs the baptism of the Holy Spirit. The greatest proof of our need for the Spirit is the state of the churches today. Hundreds are closed and countless others carry on a religion with no converts or revivals. Human logic cannot convince the unsaved that he is a sinner. Only the Holy Spirit can do this. Besides, Paul realized that it was folly to try to combat spiritual forces of evil with human weapons. He wrote to the Ephesians (Chapter 6): 'Finally, my brethren, be strong in the Lord, and in the power of his might. For we wrestle not against flesh and blood, but against principalities, against powers, against the rulers of the darkness in this world, against spiritual wickedness in high places.'

3 Be ready to receive

When the disciples were baptized in the Holy Spirit, the multitudes which had assembled cried out: 'Men and brethren, what shall we do?' (Acts Chapter 2, verse 37). To which Peter replied: 'Repent, and be baptized every one of you in the name of Jesus Christ for the remission of sins, and ye shall received the gift of the Holy Ghost.' There is only one sin that can keep anyone away from God, and that is the sin he will not confess. David says (Psalm 66): 'If I regard iniquity in my heart, the Lord will not hear me'. Anyone who is willing to make a full and complete surrender to Christ has the promise of 1 John Chapter 1, verse 19: 'If we confess our sins, he is faithful and just to forgive us our sins, and to cleanse us from all unrighteousness.'

4 Ask faithfully

Many Christians have been willing to make a full confession of their sin and to ask God for the Holy Spirit, but they have been unwilling to believe that God would keep His word. A faithless prayer is of little value. When a sinner comes for salvation, the devil will try to place doubt in their mind: 'You are too big a sinner' or 'You have stayed away from God too long.' The sinner receives an experience when he takes a firm stand on the Word of God and he refuses to heed those doubts. Every attack of the enemy must be resisted with the Sword of the Spirit.

5 Yield yourself

In his letter to the Romans (Chapter 6, verse 13) Paul says, 'Yield yourselves unto God.' No matter how far someone may go with God into the heights of spiritual experience, God never deprives them of their natural will, which remains capable of showing obedience or disobedience. Even when someone is baptized in the Holy Spirit with such evidence as the speaking in tongues, the Spirit of God has not taken possession, but rather they have given him possession.

6 Pay the price

Salvation is the gift of God and certainly cannot be bought. Yet certain conditions must be met before it becomes our possession. The rich young ruler who came running to Jesus with an earnest desire for eternal life went away sad, simply because he was unwilling to pay the price of giving up all to become the follower of Jesus. Although Jesus gave the command to at least 500 to wait until they were endued with power from on high, only 120 obeyed the command. Although the promise of God is to pour out His Spirit upon all flesh in the last days, the Word of God has clearly stated that many will refuse God's offer of pardon and power.

7 Walk in the Spirit

To the Galatians, Paul wrote: 'If you have been filled with the Spirit, then walk in the Spirit.' It is one thing to be filled with the Spirit; quite another to walk in the Spirit. The Holy Spirit comes to guide the believer into all truth; but how can He accomplish this ministry in the life of a believer who will not study the Word of Truth? The Holy Spirit comes to give us power to witness; but how can He empower the testimony of someone who neglects to witness? Baptism in the Holy Spirit represents divine equipment placed at the disposal of the believer by the Lord. To use this equipment wisely according to the divine pattern is to produce the fruit of the Spirit. To neglect to use what God has given brings only reproach, not only to the believer, but often and unjustly to the Holy Spirit.

8 Understand the gift of tongues

To be baptized in the Holy Spirit is to be immersed in Him and completely given over to Him. The two faculties which are the last to be handed over are the mind and the tongue. Almost from earliest childhood, children will manifest a will and a determination which does not want to be broken. But in speaking in an unknown tongue, the mind and the tongue are given over completely to the Holy Spirit; for in 1 Corinthians Chapter 4, verse 14, Paul says: 'If I pray in an unknown tongue, my spirit prayeth.' Paul clearly discriminates between the gift of tongues, which is a message directed by the Spirit to the people of the entire congregation that might be edified; and the speaking with other tongues in praising and praying in one's own private, devotional life. God does not give every baptized believer the gift of tongues and the gift of interpretation, any more than he would give to every Spirit filled Christian the gift of miracles and the gifts of healing. There are many who have been baptized in the Holy Spirit, with speaking in other tongues, and have continued to enjoy a prayer life of praying and praising God in the unknown tongue, who have never exercised the gift of tongues by bringing a message publicly to the rest of the congregation.

9 Pray in an unknown tongue

Certainly speaking in the unknown tongue is not the only phase of the Holy Spirit's ministry in the life of the baptized believer. But if it touches the believer's prayer life, it is touching one of the most important elements in his existence. Great men have been great because they have been great in prayer. In speaking of prayer, Paul defines two types of praying. On the one hand, there is praying with the understanding, when the mind guides the prayer in asking God for petitions that the heart desires; and on the other, praying in the unknown tongue, when the Spirit guides the prayer in an utterance unknown to the human mind. Paul writes: 'For if I pray in an unknown tongue, my spirit prayeth, but my understanding is unfruitful. What is it then? I will pray with the spirit, and I will pray with the understanding also' (1 Corinthians Chapter 14, verse 15). Praying in the unknown tongue is launching further into the spiritual realm, where the Holy Spirit guides the prayer and the utterance according to His own will.

It should have been no surprise to me that in a little while the Lord was leading me into a calling, the work He had mapped out for me. He had begun to equip me for this colossal challenge. This did not mean, though, that I was immediately willing to do everything He wanted – especially if it meant taking a blind step into the unknown. . . .

7   A Reluctant Healer

*Prepare thy work without and make it fit for thyself
in the field and then afterwards build thine house*
                  – Proverbs Chapter 24 verse 27

My mind was spinning as I walked down the street
towards the Masons's Hall in Horncastle, a tiny Lincolnshire town. It was a warm April evening in the early
1960s. Very unusually for early Spring, the sun shone
brightly and everything was quiet in the sleepy country
town. Months before I had received a letter of invitation
to conduct a two week mission to this small town of just
over 3,000 people. Local ministers on the Assemblies of
God council had planned an initiative to reach and plant
a number of churches in this county, the second largest
in the United Kingdom. They were concerned that there
were so many towns on the East Coast which had little
or no evangelistic witness.

But the first preacher they invited had got himself
double-booked and they had turned to me as the nearest
young minister (at that time I was living at Spilsby, ten
miles away). Perhaps nobody else wanted to do it, I
pondered as I walked. After all, even I had heard about
the two-week mission that had previously been staged
here; it lasted just five days because no one turned up.
What had I taken on?

I had not approached the mission lightly. I had
fasted and prayed much, and I felt the heaviness of
the responsibility, both to my fellow pastors who had
helped finance the outreach, and to the townspeople
who were expecting someone with a gift of healing.

But above all I was anxious not to let God down, that this might be a good witness for Jesus and for the faith before the eyes of the world. In the face of all this I felt very unworthy.

I made my way to the hall and up the many steps, for it was an 'upper room' hall on the second floor. The kitchen had been prepared as a vestry, and I spent some time in prayer while volunteer workers set out the chairs. The hall was empty.

My final prayers were interrupted by Charlie, a personal friend, who came in and headed for a stack of chairs in the corner for the kitchen.

'What on earth do you need more chairs for, Charlie?'

'Because we're packed, Melvin! Every place is taken and we need to squeeze some more seating in. They're standing down the stairs and out in the street waiting to get in.' He sounded as astonished as I was.

How we got them all in I don't know. But what a night it was! I preached my first ever crusade sermon (on John Chapter 14: 'Heaven and how to get there'), and these quiet country people responded. When I made the appeal, eighteen people came up to receive Christ. And the singing and the music and the testimonies – all were magnificent.

And it went on night after night. There was heartache at first, for the healings seemed to happen much more slowly than the conversions. But there was a breakthrough in the second week, with some clear cases of sick, crippled people getting instant relief and healing. People left and came back the next night, with no pain, no crippled joints, no arthritis.

The last night came, and the hall was packed. I announced the start of a new church, right in the town centre, in a nice hall just off the market square. Later we were able to purchase this, and later still, as the congregation grew, we took over the Conservative district headquarters. Today, there are two churches in the town. It was a good start to a life as an evangelist and healer.

But it was a shaky one. I started out a very reluctant healer, and certainly had no intention of making a career of it. But God thrust it upon me. Another invitation arrived at the manse in Spilsby. Then another. I held one mission; then another – each achieving some more success, further healings, greater blessings, more interest in our message and our Lord's miraculous powers. God was being merciful when He gave me such a gradual entry into such a ministry, for I might well have run away, like Jonah, had I known what was in store: the healing of multitudes, the conversion of thousands, the establishment of new churches, the television and radio shows, the scrutiny of the media, the demanding fasting and prayer times, the long hours of counselling, writing, studying, preparing, the endless queues of incurably sick people, the spiritual warfare, the jealousy of fellow ministers, the months of long travel. . .

I felt – still feel – unworthy for the task God had planned for me. I felt myself to be unlearned, untalented, unfit, unable to cope with the work that lay before me. But God can use whomever He chooses, whenever He chooses, in whatever way He chooses. It does not do to get a swelled head when God chooses you for something, because He has used some mighty strange people in the past.

The important thing is to listen for the call. It can come in many ways: by the Word of God as you read the Bible; by personal individual assurance; by a deep conviction that you can do nothing else; by circumstances pushing you in one particular direction; by the conviction of your husband or wife; by the agreement of your family or friends. But when it comes, go! Do not say, 'I will obey when I'm ready.' Eleanor Roosevelt used to say, 'If we wait till we're ready, we never do anything.' After all, God knows when we are ready and He will not say 'go' until we are.

Another thing to remember is that His call is an individual one. He calls each person to a different work, and it is a grave mistake to try to conform ourselves into a pattern we see in others. How obviously wrong this is, but how difficult to avoid! I can often tell where a particular Christian comes from by the way they talk, the jargon they use, even by the way they move.

It is just as bad to expect others to fit into a mould. I remember a man coming up to me at the end of a service in Manchester a few years ago, very angry that I had allowed a collection to be taken at my meeting. I explained that it was for our missionary crusades. He declared that I should be like George Mueller (no doubt his hero) and just pray and wait for the cash to come flying in through the window.

'But I don't have George Mueller's sort of faith', I replied.

'Well, you should get George Mueller's sort of faith', he retorted.

'The Bible says we should have the faith of God', I answered, mildly. I then asked him how many miracles of healing George Mueller had worked? None, he said.

'Did George Mueller have the sort of faith to open the eyes of the blind? No. Did he make the paralysed walk? No. Did he cause the deaf to hear? No.

'But not because he had no faith. It was because he had no gift of healing. But what he did have was the faith to get thousands of orphans fed. I couldn't help orphans, not without asking other Christians to help. But Mueller had the strength of faith to see it done. For my part, I have the naked faith to see definite miracles of healing for thousands of people, and to see it put into practice.'

The man slipped away quietly.

The call to be an evangelist is a special one, not least at this time. Britain, Europe, even the USA, have become dormant in the matter of evangelism. And yet other parts of the world, particularly in the Far East, are experiencing a spiritual revival. In his book *Revival Fire* Charles Finney has written some sobering words:

'There is a tendency to conclude that the churches can exist and prosper as well without revivals as with them. This is certainly the most preposterous conclusion conceivable. . . Leading men of the Church seem ready to make 'no effort to promote revivals and even discountenance the labours of evangelists. The Christian Church cannot survive without revivals. . . . The policy of frowning on special efforts in revival, if not arrested, must end in ruin for the Church.'

* * *

God called me, and I have not deviated from His path in my response. I might have begun reluctantly and hesitantly, but God has given me confidence, step by step.

Soon we carried the Gospel into seaside resorts, villages, cities, towns and estates; from the Highlands of Scotland to the toe of Cornwall. We have travelled from the lakes of Cumbria to the green fields of Kent; from the slums of Liverpool to the flatlands of Lincolnshire; from the recessionist North to the affluent South; from the Calvinistic Scottish islands to the Arminian West of England; from the ghettoes of Brixton to the rich coasts of Torquay; from the Roman Catholic Falls Road to the Protestant valleys of Wales. And all along, I have been discovering that:

As we uplift the Cross, the windows of Heaven open to prayer.
As we uplift the Cross, there is healing for the wounds, the diseases, the suffering of the people;

As we uplift the Cross, the broken are restored;
As we uplift the Cross, there is relief of conscience
and peace of heart and mind;
As we uplift the Cross, people's souls are purged
from sin, guilt and even the stains are washed
away.

8 *The Amazing Prophecies*

Their time, their thrills are mine
                                        – D.H. Lawrence

One of the most neglected of the spiritual gifts mentioned in the Bible is the gift of prophecy. I have a lot of respect for this one, since it was a remarkable 'rub' with an outstanding prophet which helped change the whole direction of my life.

I had been holding a healing mission with a small band of people at a large northern seaside town in the middle of summer. The town attracted some half million visitors and locals, so it was an ideal spot. But I was most impressed by the great faith of the tiny church which had sponsored our visit. The mission was a great success, turning into a mini-revival, and many were saved and many healed through our Lord Jesus Christ.

At the end, before I left for my home in Spilsby, I spent an hour with Roger Tearle, the pastor of the small church. Suddenly, he jumped up from the table and declared:

'I have a word from the Lord for you!'

'Go on, then,' I replied, 'I am prepared to hear and trust what you have to say.' I had had a couple of over-emotional people try this on me before, with little result. But I had worked with Roger through the previous eight days and had come to respect his faith and his spiritual maturity.

He began by speaking in other tongues for a little while. Then he announced:

'You are going to expand beyond your wildest dreams. You will go forth, in a little while, to the little islands and people, small folk: they need your help. You will soon leave your church. You will have a new home in a new part of the country. I will send you many helpers; many will assist you. You must take your roots from where you are and move from that place to the place where the Lord will plant you.

'You will have upheaval. The Lord will take care of everything.'

Although I had grown to love Roger, I thought he must have a 'long' imagination. As I travelled back to Spilsby, I thought how happy I was in my work. For twelve years I had built up the work, and first Lincolnshire and now the whole of the east coast of England was opening up. We were becoming well known as a centre of evangelism, and there were signs that even greater growth was in store. Besides, I knew no one outside Britain; indeed, I had only made a few short trips to France and one to the USA, and that was all my experience of life abroad. I had no personal vision for any nation apart from Britain and felt I was an evangelist for this country alone. Many of the details in Roger's prophecy simply could not be true, I decided.

I had been home for a week or so, when one of the elders of my church rang me. He wanted to see me urgently.

'Melvin,' he said when he arrived, 'we cannot sustain the vision any longer.' I looked at him, amazed. 'It's like this', he went on slowly. 'For twelve years we have come with you all the way. The miracles, the blessings of God, have been great. But the sacrifice has been great too. Financially, the weight upon the church has become intolerable. We find, as elders, that it is time to rest, slacken the pace, fortify and keep what has come in. The growth rate has been large: we need to slow down and take stock.

'This means you can be released to go out and work on your own. You can leave the church and perhaps another leader could come in to pastor, to strengthen the work. There is a need for a parting of the ways.'

I was flabbergasted. How could these men quit now, after such blessing of the work, such revival? They had been with me through thick and thin. They were good, faithful men. But now, to change course just when were winning. . . . It beat me.

The next few days saw long hours of discussions, but the elders would not change their minds. I lost patience with them and thought they had gone mad! But the consequences for us were worse than I had at first realized. A few nights later Lilian told me that one of the elders had said to her that day that we would have to vacate the manse. We could stay for six months or so, but really they wanted the house as soon as possible.

The horror of it began to dawn on me. Here we were, having collected thousands of pounds for pioneering churches but with no money we could call our own, no church, no base for our ministry, no financial backers – it felt like the end of our work.

Then I remembered Roger's prophecy, given less than a month before: 'You will have upheaval. . .you must take up your roots and move to the place where the Lord will plant you.' But where could we go? Although dozens of churches would have opened their doors for me to be their preacher or their pastor, what church could share my vision and take on a minister who spent eight months a year away from the church, winning souls elsewhere?

Late one Sunday night, Lilian and I were going over it all yet again: no job, no house, no money, no church. . . . Then Lilian declared:

'I'm going to ring your mother. She said something some months ago about your Uncle Percy selling his last house.' Percy had had a lot of property and this was the last piece he was selling. But how could I ask him for favours, when my only contact with him for the last fifteen years had been a brief meeting each New Year? Besides, how could we pay for a house with nothing? It was now midnight, and I said, 'Leave it till tomorrow, or give it a few days.' But Lilian was insistent that she rang there and then.

She did. Mother took some minutes getting out of bed and down the stairs to the phone, but she finally lifted the receiver and answered sleepily. Lilian explained our difficulties, that we were really at the end of the road. Mother replied with love and gentleness and told us not to worry: she would speak to Uncle Percy. And she would pray.

The next day she rang back with astonishing news. Two buyers for the house were due to arrive at my uncle's within the hour, offering cash for a quick sale. But Percy would turn them both down if we wanted the house. More than that, we could have it for half-price *and* he would give us three years to pay him back. The house needed some work doing to it, but they would help pray the money in. The prophecy was being fulfilled!

I was able to pay Uncle Percy back in eighteen months, and from then on we had our very own, permanent, base. Today our brand new office in Wiltshire sees tens of thousands of tracts, books and other literature going out across the world. Each year I visit as many as a dozen countries on missionary and church-planting campaigns, but many people come to see me at the office and prayer centre. Closer to home, too, the move has also given us the opportunity to plant churches in the dormant West of England – some ten churches in the past few years.

Concerning the prophecy, we learnt that God never speaks without fulfilling His word to us. Two parts of the prophecy had come true. Now we were to experience the expansion of our ministry which God had promised, as doors opened all around the world.

9   *Open Doors*

*A man's gift maketh room for him and bringeth
him before. . .men*

King Solomon

As the gift of healing has become more accepted in the
Church and in the outside world, I have been amazed
and humbled by the many doors which God has opened
to me. For instance, I have recently spent seven weeks
in Australia, New Zealand and the Pacific. During that
time I took part in almost seventy television and radio
programmes – including the popular 'Good Morning
Australia' breakfast show – and was the subject of
some thirty newspaper articles, reports and interviews.
Through this means the Gospel of Christ was brought
to some four million people. Every year I am given the
opportunity to confront millions of people in the UK
and overseas with the marvels of God.

A typical challenge these days is to heal people 'on
air'. One particular radio station in the Pacific has done
this four times now. On the first three occasions they
brought along four or five sick people, and as I prayed,
God healed them one by one, live. Almost all of them
went away well.

The last time, the radio people must have been thinking
'we must stop him somehow'. They reasoned that if
I healed only one out of a group of sick people I
had 'won' somehow. So, to reduce the odds they
presented me with just one badly-crippled woman.
I had had some idea of what they were up to,
and had spent many hours in prayer, quietness and

solitude before going to the studio. I said to the Lord:

'You cannot fail, whether it's one person or fifty. You love every one of the sick. Touch this badly crippled lady.'

The red light in the studio came on, and after some music and a few questions, the poor woman was wheeled in. I prayed, and before long she was rejoicing and dancing round the studio! The media folk were more flabbergasted than before!

But I am constantly being astonished by the opportunities God gives me, the doors He opens. . .

I preach at a Hindu temple

During a crusade in a big tent in Wellingborough, bus loads of Hindus came from miles around. It started with Patel, a little Hindu girl who had been brought by some Asian friends in a car from Leicester. She was six and had never walked in her life. A family friend had chanced to see a poster about the crusade, and though they knew nothing about the healing power of the Holy Spirit and had never been to a Christian meeting before, they came.

At the end of the meeting I laid hands on Patel, a poor, sickly child, and I felt great love and compassion filling my heart. Within five minutes of prayer, even these normally quiet and subdued Asians were jumping and shouting and hugging each other as little Patel trotted up the aisle, her thin, weak legs getting stronger by the minute.

This let the lid off the kettle, as they say, and soon mini-buses and large coaches were coming from all over, full of Asian folk with sick friends and relatives. One big coachful arrived from Leicester an hour and a half before the service. Never before had there been such a movement among Asians in the

South Midlands, never before such openness to the Gospel.

As a result, I was approached by a prominent Asian businessman in Leicester, a strong Hindu, and asked if I would visit their temple and pray for the sick. I wrote back saying that my healing ministry could not be separated from the Gospel of Jesus, the saviour of all 'for there is none other name under heaven given amongst men, whereby we must be saved'.

I expected no reply, but soon received an excited phone call:

'I have talked to our leaders. They are happy for you to come. You can preach what you want, we don't mind. We need God's power through you.'

How could I resist such an opportunity? – even though none of the local Christians seemed to appreciate it as such. I found no back-up from the churches in the area, despite this being an unheard of offer. One church leader, whom I knew well as being keen on mission, sending missionaries out to India and Pakistan, nevertheless failed to offer any help. That was his Bible study night, he explained!

Undaunted, Lilian and I pressed ahead and arrived at the businessman's house in a wealthy Leicester suburb, where we were to spend the night before the mission. That evening, over a hot curried chicken with rice, I learnt many things about hospitality I have never forgotten and I was able to talk to our hosts about Jesus. We slept well, and spent the morning praying hard for the two services which were to take place in the afternoon and evening.

I was not speaking in the Hindu shrine itself, but in a community hall which was part of the temple complex. When we arrived half an hour before the first service, the street was already full of people in turbans, women in sarees, little children, mothers carrying sick infants. I was shown into the hall by courteous guides and soon the place was full with some 700 people, interested, hungry, curious. I spoke through a young woman interpreter for about forty-five minutes about Christ, the only mediator between man and God; how He shed His blood to forgive us our sins for ever; how He died; how He rose again on the third day – Hallelujah!

At the end, there was hardly one person who did not raise their hand and pray the sinner's prayer. Many could not do it with a dry eye. And scores were healed, the blind saw, cripples walked, little babies were made well again.

The evening service was equally well attended, and afterwards Lilian and I walked out tired, sad that the local churches had missed the chance to jump in with support and follow-up. . .but thrilled at the great work God had begun among the Hindus that night.

The poor rich man

In Zurich, Switzerland, I had the opportunity to talk to a multi-millionaire. There were plenty of "doors" for God to open that night, for it took me a full half-hour to get around the Dobermanns, through all the electronic doors, past all the security checks and under the secret cameras which surrounded his securely-guarded house. And this was just one of the houses he had scattered around the major cities of Europe.

I finally passed the test and, leaving my shoes at the door, walked across magnificent Persian carpets into his presence. He shook my hand warmly and we sat down, he with a whisky, me with an orange juice. I caught myself marvelling at how I, a simple, unworthy preacher, could be brought by God into contact with such a rich, powerful man. He told me about the futility of his life, his emptiness, his forlornness. He told me how he felt no security, no peace – indeed, how poor his life was.

I in turn told him about the thrills and joys of knowing Jesus. I told him what God could do for him. It was perhaps the first, perhaps the only, chance he had to hear the glories of salvation offered to him through our blessed Lord.

Sadly, he turned down the chance. I have been able to witness our Lord heal many life-threatening diseases, but on that occasion was unable to heal him of his riches. He clung instead to his sinful pleasures, unwilling to give up his idols and seek first God's kingdom.

£3,000 for a healing

Also in Switzerland there lived a millionairess, who contacted me a few years ago asking me to go and pray for her. In return, I was offered a plane ticket, a hotel room for the night, a chauffeur to pick me up from the airport – and £3,000. I was pioneering new churches on a shoestring budget and really needed all the money I could get.

I had no thought of personal gain, but getting the money for the work of the Gospel was a great temptation. And yet there came a clear leading in my conscience that it was not right. I spoke to the woman and prayed for her on the phone that she would be healed, but never accepted her generous offer. The gifts of God are free. Indeed, they are without price. I was poorer financially for that decision, but richer in every other way. *And* the woman's condition improved from that night on.

The drug-addicts' church

It was a small congregation in the community centre of an old German town. That morning I had preached at a huge Pentecostal meeting of some three to four hundred people, but here, just thirty miles away on a crisp January afternoon, were some forty young married couples and their children. Their pastor told me the story of this remarkable group.

Less than a year earlier, nearly everyone there had been a hardened drug addict. Most were well-educated and many had once held good jobs. But then they had opted out, started living together, got interested in eastern religions and become hooked on cocaine, barbiturates, even glue. Some, though, had wanted to kick the habit, and one day three of them decided:

'Right, let's try this guy Jesus. We see His figure [the crucifix] outside the churches.' And so, unprompted, they began to pray: 'O Jesus, fellow, if you're there somewhere in the cosmos, help us. . .'

They wept, they cried, they called until, one after another, they felt a presence, a power, an assurance. Peace came to them, all at once, and they began to weep in earnest, and laugh, and jump around the room. Later, they found an old Bible and began to realize what had happened to them. And fortunately a young Scandinavian preacher was in Germany at the time and bumped into them 'by accident'. He was able to give them the basic Bible teaching they needed.

And now here I was a year later, standing before the fruits of that first conversion. The news of their miraculous change had spread quickly and others in their alternative community came forward to be delivered. Those not married were wed, families came back together, love grew, eastern religions were abandoned, drugs were given up. When I arrived there was a lot of noise – chairs scraping, children running about, doors banging. But as soon as they settled down, all opened their Bibles and fixed their eyes on me. Speaking through an interpreter I gave the longest sermon I have ever preached – nearly two hours on the truths of the Christian faith. And almost the only sound was the rustle as they turned the pages of their Bibles.

When it was over it was quite late and I was due at another church that evening. But it was a long time before I could tear myself away. They hugged me, they crowded round, asked questions – even produced an 'English tea' with lovely German gateaux. Later we were able to arrange for a fine, pioneering German-speaker from Switzerland to go and minister to them. I have been back there many times, each time with a sense of privilege at being able to visit such a remarkable, growing church.

Miracles in a crematorium

A well-known TV celebrity once contacted me and asked if I could conduct his mother's funeral. A few years earlier I had seen him healed of a dreadful hernia at one of my meetings. I accepted, but with trepidation, for in nearly twenty-five years of ministry up to that time I had only conducted about three funerals. I don't know, it seemed everyone in our churches lived for ever. I heard that people came to our church because they could be sure of staying healthy and living a good long time!

Anyway, when I turned up at the crematorium, I found the place packed with a large crowd of familiar figures from the showbiz world. The TV celebrity was well-respected, and many actors, musicians and performers had come on his account. I had one of the most marvellous opportunities to present the Good News about Jesus Christ to people who were in the main far from God, lost in their careers, fame, riches and ambition. For half an hour I preached that all ought to repent; I warned of hell; and I urged them to make a real commitment of their lives, in the belief that the Holy Spirit would regenerate them. In the quiet closing moments one hand after another was raised to ask for peace and salvation through the shed blood of Christ.

Afterwards, at the funeral lunch, a number came up to me and told how they had been touched in their hearts (by the Spirit of God). One famous star said the last time he had been to a Christian service was during a visit by Billy Graham to London. He had not responded at the time and had never thought he would have had the chance to make his peace with God. Now he felt his life had changed. It was a sad day for my friend in a way, but also a wonderful day of comfort, hope and power.

Preaching in a Muslim's nightclub

My local organizer was getting desperate, trying to find a church in Gloucester for our meetings. Despite a good press, a good record of conversions, and a good name in the city, he could get no interest from the churches there. He looked for a vacant hall. Still no success.

One day, one of my friends was talking to a Muslim who owned a nightclub.

'What a shame you cannot find a place', said the Muslim. 'Why not come here?'

Surely, we thought, people would not come to such a sordid place for healing. But they did. We had three services there on a day in the middle of the week and four hundred people turned up. One hundred and thirty were saved, and one man literally leapt from a wheelchair and ran around the club. God worked in a Muslim's nightclub, and put the churches to shame.

A publican gets to heaven

A similar problem occurred in a small West Country town. Our visit had been long expected and there was great anticipation. Our phone was busy with people making enquiries, and many sick people were being brought in from miles around.

One day, shortly before the mission was due to start, I came home to find an urgent telephone message from our organizer in the town. I rang anxiously and finally got through on his busy line.

'Lots of people ringing in, Melvin', he reported. 'Marvellous interest, many non-Christians want to come and hear you preach. Loads of people asking for help, prayer and details of the service. Only, we have this problem: the church has taken fright and opted out. We can't hold the service there.'

I could not believe it. It was supposed to be an evangelical, Bible-believing church, pleading for the unsaved to come to church and find God. And here it was, turning them away when they wanted to come! We scratched around every inch of ground in that town, but we could find no other hall within two miles of the town centre that seemed to be available. It looked as if we would have to cancel. Then the organizer came on the phone again, excited this time:

'We have a hall!'

'How on earth did you do it?', I asked, amazed.

'Oh, I got the pub', he replied.

'The pub?!'

It turned out to be a large room behind the main bar. The publican, when I met him, was smoking a big cigar and greeted me warmly.

'Well, there was no room at the inn for *Him*, was there', he smiled. 'So we'd better make up for it this time, hadn't we? And seeing it's your church that has no room for Him this time, we couldn't say no, could we?'

Thanks to his act of hospitality, the mission went ahead. Three hundred came and a hundred were converted. Great miracles were performed, and people went home pushing empty wheelchairs, carrying their sticks and with their dark glasses and hearing aids in their pockets. Afterwards, I thanked the publican:

'And what did you think of the action?'

'I was very happy to have you here', he replied.

'When we welcome the Gospel message into our homes, there can only be God's blessing on it.'

'Well, I didn't turn you away, did I?'

'And if you take Jesus in,' I responded, 'He will make all the difference to your life.'

'You must be right', he agreed. 'I am nearer than ever before. I didn't reject Him, did I?'

I left town, and three weeks later heard that the publican had died in a car accident. I sent a message to his wife, who said she was greatly comforted by it. One of the quotes I sent was, 'This is my son who was dead and is alive again; was lost and is now found.'

* * *

In all this, I remember that I am just a simple Wiltshire preacher. But God pushes me into the pathways of so many different people and gives me a Gospel to proclaim. I thank Him always for the way that firmly closed doors swing wide open at His bidding.

10   *West Wales Revival*

Who is she that looketh forth as the morning, fair as the moon, clear as the sun and terrible as an army with banners?

Song of Solomon

I had no idea what I was stepping into that Saturday night as I drove through the streeets of Gorseinon, looking for the 'Miracle Tabernacle', the church which had invited me to this small Welsh town for some crusade meetings. But God whispered to me:

'Love these people. I will give you extra power, for this is the day of My power. Do not judge people by their attitudes, nor by their shortcomings: I will send you all sorts of people. You will need Me with you. I will empower you.'

I wondered what was coming. Little did I know that *a real Revival was about to begin!*

I had always loved the Welsh people anyway, especially since my mother and grandparents, aunts and cousins were all Welsh. But I had found it the hardest part of Britain. In England, Scotland and Ireland I have reaped such a harvest of souls. But the response in Wales was only a fraction compared with these other countries. It always took twice as much time, prayer and effort, even to get a small harvest there. But I sensed something in that opening meeting that I had never found in any part of Wales before.

Soon, right in that first meeting, *sixty* people were converted – an amazing response for the principality. Soon hundreds were coming to the knowledge that they were born again.

I fell in love with these Welsh-speaking people. Soon they were singing the old choruses, and they rang through the town as news of the miracles spread: 'There is power, power, wonder-working power in the Blood of the Lamb.'

We moved into a new sphere of God, grasping at the promise of revival. The area was shaken by the glory of God: goitres vanished, sicknesses of every type disappeared. God gave me a new realization of faith. Many began to speak with new tongues; some fell to the ground like a pack of cards; cripples found legs grown; heart diseases were righted. . . . We could feel God everywhere, even in the streets. People wept, the meetings lasted long hours, few wanted to go home, people danced for joy, wept, laughed, loved each other. Evil spirits were addressed by the word of authority and power, and driven out. The mighty word of God fell from my lips with power I had not known before, melting and shattering the icy grip of unbelief, piercing open the wounds of sin.

I had to go off to other meetings elsewhere, but I returned as soon as I could. I found hundreds upon hundreds had been saved, healed, filled with the Holy Spirit. It was truly a revival!

Soon the blind, deaf, paralysed, broken, sick, were being healed left, right and centre. There were long queues, the patients praying, people getting healed, worshipping even while they waited for up to three hours. Sixteen people in wheelchairs came to one meeting alone, brought by a line of ambulances. Eight nurses came one night to bring the sick and three were saved on the spot, even though they had only come to do their job. Many walked from their wheelchairs, and sticks, crutches, walking frames, neck braces, hearing aids, callipers, glasses were discarded. One lady – Mrs Grasse – experienced a complete healing from arterial heart disease and has been declared by her doctors to be in perfect health.

It was out of this world! People got saved before the meetings started. Folk were made well on the way to the meetings. It was incredible!

Nevertheless, many churches were passed by in West and South Wales, for the blessing broke out only among a small group of Pentecostal people, devout, holy, Spirit-filled, earnest, prayerful. They found that God had chosen them for His great work there.

The reason at the centre of the West Wales visitation (as well anyone can judge) was the strong emphasis on the proclamation of Calvary. And in the follow-up, the good church growth has been due to establishing the converts in the Word, in prayer, Bible-studies, all with a strong emphasis on the finished work of Calvary and the blood of Jesus. But where in these days can be found the conditions necessary for a mighty work of God? It can only be where the Atonement of Christ is proclaimed and the Scriptures accepted sincerely as the Word of the living God.

In the little principality of Wales, these conditions can still be found. Generally speaking, the pulpit has been true to the Evangelical faith in all its essentials, and the Gospel of the grace of God has been faithfully preached to the people. The nation has clung to the faith of its fathers, the exception being the few who have been touched by the spirit of cynicism and unbelief so prevalent in other lands. True, people may be living in the traditions of the past, but there has not been a departure from the faith 'once for all delivered to the saints'. Wales has also had special advantages in its Sunday Schools, where people of all ages gather to learn the Word of God, and earnest efforts are directed to make the teaching effectual by systematic study and examinations. Although there has been much decline, the background of faithful groups of prayerful, born-again people, plus the growth of 'renewed' churches and house meetings – all have played a part in nudging West Wales towards a revival breakthrough.

The word 'revival' is used forty times in Scripture. In Greek it is *anozuno* – 'to come back to life' or 'to fan into a flame', as in Paul's words to Timothy: 'Stir up the gift that is within thee', stir it up into flames. In Hebrew the word is *kawya* or *kaya*, meaning 'to restore' or 'recover' or 'be made whole again'. Thus Habbakuk prayed: 'Revive thy work; recover it, restore it so the earth will be full of your praise.'

In England I had been close to such a revival before. But the English apathy has been a great hindrance to revival. We get a bit of a blessing and we withdraw, get self-satisfied. Billy Graham comes, or Reinhardt Bonke, or Luis Palau, and things get stirred up. But then it is all allowed to slip away because of our half-heartedness. We get tired quickly, lose energy, get apathetic.

Pastors are to blame as much as their congregations. I had a church write to me: 'We do not need any more evangelistic crusades now. We have reached one hundred members.' And yet they were in a town of 75,000 people, and they were almost the only evangelistic church there! Another pastor wrote: 'We have had so many converts since your crusade in our church, can you cancel your next visit until two years ahead? We cannot manage any more new people at the moment. Our hands are full.'

What a disgrace! How can you have revival with such an attitude? In Wales and throughout the world, God is wanting to raise up a new breed of believer: anointed, hungry, dedicated, saved, thankful; not self-satisfied, settled, cautious, but holy, on fire, with drive, love and *passion*. Revival is more than good evangelism and needs more commitment. It is the righteousness of God breaking out beyond human control. The Church in England has been like 22,000 football fans, badly in need of exercise, watching and cheering on twenty-two football players, who are badly in need of a rest! The

73

Church is still largely a non-participator.

One little lady well into her nineties had clear memories of Evan Roberts and the great Welsh Revival in 1904. Speaking of our new work, she told me:

'This is the greatest revival, the most powerful harvest of souls in this part of Wales since that time. God has come again!'

God came to Wales again through his Holy Spirit at that time. The years since then have shown the greatest church growth since before the First World War. Deep in the roots of this new revival lies the work we saw God begin in this part of Wales.

11   *Slowboat to China*

The music I heard with you, was more than music, and the bread I broke with you was more than bread

Joseph Conrad

The phone rang in our Chippenham crusade office one Monday in Summer 1980. I was just leaving for some meetings in the West Midlands, so one of my staff answered. They called out:

'Can you wait a minute? There's a minister who has come eight thousand miles especially to see you. Can you give him a few moments?'

I was in a great hurry, but this intrigued me. I often had calls from ministers in Europe, but nobody from this distance before. What on earth did he want, I wondered.

'I have been looking for you, Reverend Bank,' said a soft-spoken voice in broken English. 'Kindly, some pastors told me where you lived, but said that it would be almost impossible to catch you.'

'But what can I do for you?', I asked.

'I believe the Lord wants you to come and preach to the Chinese people of South-East Asia.'

I was flabbergasted!

'Listen, I'm just leaving for a mission,' I told the person, 'but I shall be back in four days.' There was a moment's silence; then the voice came back, excitedly:

'That is very good, Reverend Bank! That will be my last day in England. My flight back to Asia is the next day. I will see you Friday. . .'

Four days (and one successful mission) later, I was sitting amongst the roses in my back garden, enjoying a cup of tea, when Lilian asked quietly:

'What is a Singaporean like?'

'What do you mean? What colour are they? Or what is their character? Or what?'

'Are they small people?'

I suddenly realized what she was getting at, and shot out of my chair.

'Of course! The prophecy! 'You will go forth in a little while, to the little islands and people, small folk: they need your help.' Could this be it, I wondered.

Just then, the doorbell rang. I went round the side of the house and there stood a short, plump Chinese gentleman, only about thirty years old, I guessed. His face beamed.

'Reverend Bank, I very much pleased to see you. I come very, very far to see you.' I opened the gate and led him through into the garden. 'I have been looking forward so much to meeting you, oh! afternoon tea and cakes', he exclaimed. 'I have heard English like tea and cakes in the afternoon', he went on. 'My father often thought the English mad when they ran our country of Singapore: to sit out in the midday sun with their dogs, drinking hot tea and eating hot cakes in 120 degrees!'

It was only 80 degrees but we sat in the shade and Lilian brought us tea and cream cakes. His name was Randy Singh and he explained that he had been told about my meetings: the miracles, the churches opened, the faithful service over decades. He was planning to bring together a band of some twenty young men and women, called to be evangelists with one hundred per cent dedication, and to take them through a four-month course at a college hired for the purpose. He wanted me to go and teach them for two or three weeks, and share with them the experience gained over years as an evangelist.

'Tell them how to plant churches', he went on. 'Tell them the secrets of God's miraculous powers; tell them how to be anointed by the Holy Spirit; tell them how to avoid the pitfalls, how to keep the converts, keep the people in their healing. . . . And after that,' he ended, 'perhaps you will stay for another week to hold a large crusade in Malaysia, where the people are asking for you.'

Again, the words of the prophecy, uttered three years before, rang in my ears. Tears of joy came into my eyes as I explained about it to the Chinese minister. He was silent for a moment, then said solemnly:

'What a confirmation that I have not come all this way on a wasted journey. It's wonderful, wonderful', he cried. 'God spoke to you and to me.' Then he jumped to his feet, shouting 'Hallelujah!' At least that's one word we have in common, I thought.

But what about timing? I got out my diary.

'I can't come for at least a year', I told him, sadly. 'That makes it 1981.'

'What month in 1981 can you come?', he asked anxiously. 'You see, the Lord said if you could or would come, it would be in November 1981. So I booked the college premises for then.'

I gulped, and kept thumbing.

'Do you know, the only month I can make it is. . . November!' A coincidence? What do you think? We certainly thought otherwise, and wept and hugged each other, and praised God.

So began the great Far East Outreach, which has taken me to Singapore and Malaysia five times since then, with thousands reached with the Gospel and many healed.

* * *

Eighteen months later I was in Singapore, and didn't the young people draw it out of me. There were four sessions each day, starting at 7.30 a.m. and lasting until 10 at night, with only the odd break for a meal or a rest. Question after question, session after session. But I think they put as much into me as I tried to give out to them, with their love, their eagerness to learn, their zeal to win the Orient for Christ. I shall not forget the last session with them, as they pledged never to go back from their calling, and wept as I laid hands on them. Today, they are all serving the Lord across the two lands and into India, the Philippines, East Malaysia, Indonesia and China, bringing great numbers of lost souls to Christ and planting many churches.

The missions that followed in North and South Malaysia were tremendous, with crowds packed into large halls. One Sunday in a town near Kuala Lumpur, so many turned up that the pastors told them they could only attend one service that day! It was the only way to get everyone in, even though there were *five* services that day.

I was invited back again the next year, and accepted. It was by no means a slow boat to China, for God was quickening the pace in that part of the world. He was giving vision to His people, for in 1987 persecution came with the passing of strict Islamic laws. Many Christian leaders and hundreds of believers were arrested and gaoled without charge or trial. I thank God He gave me the vision and that I was able to be faithful to it while the doors remained open to the Christian message. The result is that there is a strong Church, growing rapidly. May God help us to answer His call when it comes, and without delay.

Among my many memories of my visit there was the day we had a revival meeting in a cinema. . .

Surrounded by some forty Chinese police officers I was marshalled through a thick crowd of people, crying, reaching out, holding up their children to be touched. The whole street was packed for as far as I could see, and Lilian clung to my side as the police pushed a path through, wicker canes and whips in hand. The air was filled with cries of 'Pray, pray, touch, touch.'

It was a large Chinese town outside Kuala Lumpur. Muslim law prohibited the preaching of the Christian Gospel anywhere outside a church building, but we had sought government permission to hire a cinema for two nights and, astonishingly, got it. Now we had to get inside! Many of the crowd had slept all night in the streets in order to get a good place in the queue. They had queued throughout the hot day and now were jostling to get inside the cinema. Nearly two thousand crammed into a building designed to hold seven hundred (it's a good thing the Chinese are thin, I thought). But still outside were some three or four thousand. Anywhere else I would have gone outside and spoken to them through a loud hailer, prayed for the sick, and so on. Not here, though. Such a thing was threatened with immediate arrest, deportation, perhaps months in prison, and difficulties for the local pastors.

The crowd surged again and again as we struggled through. I called to my interpreter to ask the police not to use their whips or canes against the crowd. He tried to make himself understood to the sergeant in charge, making signs in the air, and the other policemen seemed to spot him and understand. From then on they just leaned into the crowd with their broad shoulders. Soon we were squeezed through the wire fence at the side of the building and then into the building itself. What a sight met us! The place was crammed from wall to wall, with all the aisles filled and two or three in each seat. The heat was overwhelming, perhaps 120 degrees. There was no air conditioning and all the doors had to be kept shut against those outside.

I found a little space on stage behind the curtain and turned to the pastor in charge of the meeting.

'What can be done about those people outside?'

'Nothing we can do', he shook his head, despairingly. 'Against the law, against the law.'

Just then we were joined by Alan Pimlott, the gospel singer from Norwich who had come with me for the tour. His shirt collar was ruffled from where he had been dragged throught the crowd, and sweat poured down his face. But this had no effect on his beaming smile.

'All those people out there, Melvin. . .'

'Just what I was saying, Alan. Do you think. . . ?' He burst out laughing.

'I know what's coming! Muggins me', pointing to himself, 'has to go out and get arrested.'

'I can't be in two places,' I reasoned, 'and I'm committed in here. But I wonder if you or I had a quiet word with the sergeant? He is Chinese and seems sympathetic. Maybe you could persuade him to give you twenty minutes with the crowd – just to give a short sermon, pray for folk to be saved and lead them into healing.' Alan volunteered immediately and went off.

Just as the singing was beginning for the main meeting inside, Alan dashed back in. To everyone's amazement he announced:

'He's granted us twenty or thirty minutes only! I'm taking my piano accordion with me and will sing and preach to them. Just pray I don't get thrown into prison, or crushed by the crowd', he shouted to me as he rushed away.

In fact, he managed thirty-five minutes. The crowd, thousands strong, listened with hungry, upturned faces as he sang, with a second interpreter translating for him. They followed him as he moved round the outside of the cinema. Finally, he made an appeal and hundreds raised their hands, prayed the sinner's prayer and called upon the name of Jesus to be saved. Then the police sergeant, getting increasingly nervous, gave Alan a sign to stop and he made a final mass prayer for the sick. Out in the streets, cripples slowly left their crutches and sticks, people moved their paralysed limbs, others were set free from pain. All around, people clapped and shouted at these miracles.

Inside, I too had finished preaching, and a thousand people were filling in commitment cards (in Chinese) recording their decision to receive and stand up for Christ. Each card carried the pledge to go on and do a Bible study course with the Assemblies of God for six months after the crusade. (I later asked the pastor what proportion had kept their word and completed the course and he told me *ninety-five per cent*).

The next night crowds again filled the building. Hundreds more came to Jesus; hundreds more walked, jumped, laughed, spoke, saw and heard again. Jesus the healer had passed by.

* * *

On another occasion, I was called out to the jungle in southern Malaysia, fifty miles from the nearest town. I needed healing myself after being driven by the local pastor over the pot-holed, rock-strewn roads. Journey's end was the house of a Chinese planter deep in the jungle: lizards chasing up and down the walls, no bath only a hosepipe, and mosquitoes which bit me fifteen times a night. My host was a Chinese man who begged me to heal his daughter. She lay on the floor, twisted and paralysed, barely alive, a cabbage.

I looked around at the Chinese idols on the walls, and was moved by this small child.

'Tell him', I asked my interpreter, 'to renounce his idols. If he burns them up and claims Christ as his saviour, promising to follow God, then God will deliver his child.' And I quoted the Ten Commandments to him: 'Thou shalt not make thee any graven image. . .thou shalt not bow down thyself unto them, or serve them; for I the Lord thy God am a jealous God.'

The interpreter was reluctant. He was a Christian, but he knew his own culture. Tell a man to burn his idols, relics which had been handed down through his family for hundreds of years? Impossible.

'He will never do it, sir. Never. You ask too much. Pray first, sir; let the child get healed. Then he may burn them.'

'No.' I was adamant. 'This is God's work. If the man will do it, God will not fail him.'

'What if he burns these costly relics, sir, and the child does not get healed. *Then he will burn us – alive!*' But I stood my ground.

'How can God fail?'

The interpreter had no reply (of course: there was none) and he translated my request. To everyone's surprise, except mine, the man replied:

'Yes, if God's man says I must do that, I must do it.'

It took two hours to gather them up, douse them in petrol and set fire to them. But when the last one had gone into flames, I returned to the house, touched the child and proclaimed:

'By his stripes ye are healed. I adjure in the name of Jesus Christ of Nazareth: come out of her!'

The writhing, twisting child fell silent, shook her head, and was completely healed.

On my last trip to Malaysia a year later, I visited the family again and took tea with them. While I was there, the little girl came home from school. She was a normal, healthy child, and in a year had caught up with all her schooling. As the idols were burnt and the old life surrendered, a new life had come, bringing health, salvation, peace and deliverance.

* * *

Also on that last visit, before the government finally clamped down on evangelizing, I met a little old lady on the Thai-Malay border. I had just come through deep floods after a great mission to a Muslim area in the interior. Her face was wrinkled and she had a huge bundle on her back. She talked with animation in her own language, which my interpreter translated for me.

'Thank you, Reverend Banks, for coming round the world so far to tell me about Jesus. I've been trying to find God all my life and I've found Him now. Now I belong to Jesus. Thank you again. *Come back and tell our people again soon. We love you, do not forget us.*' She moved me to tears.

I have not been able to go back since. The country is closed to me (and many evangelists) for Gospel crusades. But I have never forgotten that little lady, or her people. I pray for the persecuted Chinese people in Malaysia. And one day I will return.

That visit from Randy Singh was just the start of a new development in my ministry, which has taken me literally around the world. . . .

* * *

I shall never forget the sight of the mass of Zulu people, standing in the hot sun on the seafront near Durban, South Africa. We were there for a baptism; but first came the ecstatic singing and the earnest testimonies. One young woman, not above sixteen years of age, told how she had been an anti-white activist, helping terrorists, burning down schools with petrol bombs. Two others said they had been witch doctors. Story after story – it went on for hours. Now all were repentant, loving, meek, *born again*.

What a revival! I was thrilled to be taking part in it all. We finally got to the baptism itself, and three groups with two pastors each were needed to cope with the long queues. As the people came up out of the salty water there were long shouts of praise, dancing, arms raised, worship, even drums. It was fantastic! Tears filled my eyes. God was at work, raising up a whole new generation of loving, re-created souls.

How many were baptized that day? *Seven hundred.*

It was also in Durban that I witnessed a revival meeting on an early morning train. It was at 5.30 a.m., and the station near the black shanty towns was crammed. Finally the train pulled in and the crush merely transferred itself on board. Soon, we were hurtling towards town, the start of the day's work for thousands of Zulu workers. Suddenly, I heard a man's voice at the other end of the carriage. It was a Zulu preacher, speaking loud enough for people to hear him right down the carriage. He was preaching about Jesus, how we all need Jesus, how He died, was raised again. . . .

What wonder! What power! My eyes moistened, and a tear rolled down one cheek. No one swore at him; no one shouted. Some bowed their heads, some who were facing the other way turned round to listen. One or two put out their cigarettes. What a difference from the reception you might expect on a British train! There, though, in that revival atmosphere, there was only respect, interest and earnest attention given to the word of God.

As the train emptied in Central Durban, I saw some kneeling on the carriage floor to receive Christ; some left weeping; everyone went away with satisfaction or joy on their faces. As I left, I saw the preacher joining up with others to return up the line, in order to travel back again with the next tide of workers.

* * *

In New Zealand, Lilian and I were given a great Maori welcome in their own cultural hall, where no Gospel crusade had ever been held before. There had been some disquiet about this, and some attempts to revive the old Maori spirits and pagan worship. But what a welcome!

84

After they had rubbed noses with Lilian and me (their version of shaking hands) their choir sang 'How Great Thou Art'. I have never heard it sung better anywhere in the world, and in that Maori town, fifty were born again that night and many more were delivered and healed.

* * *

Another mission was held in a small farming community in the Australian outback. There, the bars along the dusty main street were always half-full of men (no women), concentrating on their heavy drinking. Out there, a man was a man, and consequently they had a big alcoholism problem. No evangelist had come their way for fifty years, but the Assemblies of God chapel was packed. Eighteen were saved, including the wife of one of the bar owners (she had never been in a Gospel service before), and a man threw aside his crutches in order to dance and jump!

* * *

Closer to home, in Gibraltar, crowds flocked over the border from Spain to come to the meetings. On one day six hundred came and we had to have two meetings to accommodate them. Nearly 570 registered a decision for Christ, and the whole of the colony heard about the miracles performed there, through the local television, radio and press. At one meeting, I was praying for the sick, and people got too excited, pressing through the lines. Suddenly one large Spanish woman just pushed through, and I felt her pull the back of my jacket. She tugged at it, shouting and praying. Maybe she had heard of Peter's shadow in the Bible, healing those it fell across, or the miracles performed by Paul's clothes and handkerchiefs. She suddenly began to shout with joy as, amazingly, the touch of my coat brought about a miracle of healing. There was, of course, no virtue in my old jacket; but there was and is in Jesus Christ.

* * *

When I return from one of these long journeys, walk wearily up the garden path, through the front door and greet my family for perhaps the first time in weeks or months, these miracles revive me. The memory of them soon transforms and refreshes me, and reminds me constantly of the goodness and unfailing promises of God.

I like to feel that my travels – and the miracles achieved in them – have made things easier for others. There is a story of a young boy walking home one day with an old man. In those days the paths at the side of the roads were just cinder tracks, and a new load of sharp ashes had been spread during the day.

'Let's walk on the road', suggested the boy after a while, tired of stumbling through the cinders.

'No,' the old man smiled. 'we'll walk on the path. If we don't tread it smooth, the folk who come after us will have to do it.'

If my travels have done that, in any small way, then I could hope for nothing better.

12 *Miracles in the Streets of Lincoln*

Behold God exalteth by his power. Who teacheth like him? Remember that thou magnify his marvels, which men behold that every man may see it
Job (Chapter 36, verses 22, 24, 25)

Dusk was falling as I journeyed along the quiet lanes of Lincolnshire. It was March, and spread all around me were the familiar ploughed fields and rows of turnips. Familiar too, was the smell of manure in the air.

It was twelve years since I had left the county where God had given birth to my ministry. Now, having preached around the world and affected hundreds of thousands of people, I was back for my first major crusade there.

I say major, but I was really expecting something low-key and quiet. Each year, out of forty missions around the world, I try to go to two or three rural areas; and rural Lincolnshire is very quiet. Once, the whole of the county had been, I remember preaching to sixteen people in the city of Lincoln itself twenty-five years ago. But the years of pioneering work I had done during the Sixties and Seventies had paid off, and all over the county, strong churches had been built up. It was the prayers of God's people, continuing crusading and good pastoral leadership that had brought such a healthy state to so many churches.

But some areas had not been reached by the Gospel and this was one of them. Despite that, the elderly pastor who had arranged the meetings had made a point of not inviting any churches – only a handful of his own church members and, he hoped, flocks of non-Christians. I admired his faith, but could not help wondering if the old pastor was stretching things too far, relying on a completely alien, uncommitted, unchurched community to fill the large school hall every night. Oh well, I thought, it would be nice to have a change from the usual hectic pace. I could use a little peace and tranquillity, and maybe get another chapter of my current book written. How wrong could I be!

It was dark by the time I reached the small village high street. Dim street lamps revealed the old war memorial just ahead, set back from the road and planted around with spring flowers. Across the road stood a group of teenagers, and I wound the window down and called out:

'Which way to the school hall where the miracles are going to happen?' One of them wandered across, looking puzzled. Then he replied:

'Oh, that's right. I read about that and folk have been talking about it around here. Is it true? Does it really happen?'

'Well, come and see! God can do anything, you know!' He looked surprised, but grinned and gave me directions to the school.

A few hundred yards on I found the school and swung into the car park. There was one other car there, waiting with its lights on. As I got out, one of its doors opened and a voice called out,

'What time is it opening?'

'It starts in an hour and a half', I replied. 'You're early, but it won't be long.' Then I heard two pairs of feet crunching through the darkness. What? More people early? This was amazing for Lincolnshire, where even the committed had difficulty getting to church on time.

Soon, the large hall was filling up. One of the country pastors had wondered how many we would get; he was amazed when he saw that there was standing room only. Many found Jesus; many were healed. But that first evening was just a foretaste of what was to come.

There was a cold, crisp, Lincolnshire wind blowing when I stepped out of the car for the second meeting the following afternoon. But there was nothing cold about the interest. I found the hall full from wall to wall – every inch of space filled. People overflowed into the porch, many had to listen to the service from the streets outside. It was tantamount to a revival.

Some of those in wheelchairs could not get in, so I went out to pray for them as the service began, so that they would not have to wait all through it in the bitter wind. A woman instantly threw down her crutches and walked from her wheelchair. Another man could move his paralysed legs. Revival had begun in the streets outside! People came to the windows of their houses; passers-by stopped in the street to watch. And as I moved into the building, one blind person after another saw; the deaf heard; the lame walked. What a meeting! What a welcome home! Altogether, fifty were converted that day.

One of my allies was the *Lincolnshire Echo*, which took a sceptical, anti-Christian stance from the first. No mention of this being a worldwide ministry, begun in their county, which had returned to bring benefit to their people. They were just interested in a critical story, and, though they reported some of the healings, that was what they printed. But the effect was to prompt more people to attend the meetings, not fewer, and soon the hall was packed for each meeting.

I arrived early for one afternoon service. It was fortunate, for as I walked through the village, a lady shouted:

'You'd better hurry up: folk are queuing up and hammering on the door of the hall. It's cold out here, isn't it.'

I ran the rest of the way and when I got there, what should I see but the doors of the hall wide open and, already, people unable to get in. *And there were still two hours to go before the start of the meeting.* People were sitting on tables, windowsills, even the stage, and were crammed too into the side rooms and kitchens. It took me ten minutes to squeeze in myself. I made for the stage and called for calm.

By the time the service began, there were more people outside the hall than in. A note was passed to me on the stage – it was from Lilian, who had not been able to get inside herself:

'Can you come and pray for sick outside. Many wheelchairs, many cannot get in. Very cold outside.' It is a good job I am a small man, because the only way I could get out was by being lifted bodily over the heads of the crowd in the building.

As soon as I got outside I began laying hands on people. And straight away, amazing things happened, which staggered even Lilian and me. People left wheelchairs, sticks were thrown away, people shouted out that their pain was gone. . .I had seen such miracles in Britain before inside a hall, but here it was all happening out in the streets, on the sidewalks of that Lincoln suburb. Neighbours came to their doors or craned out of windows, crowds came out of the shops, people from a local factory peered over the wall, and the press came and had a field day.

Soon, the news spread, and the crowds grew bigger and the traffic blocked up. People clapped at each miracle, and there was laughter, joy and excitement – all praise to God in the open air. What an afternoon! They will never be forgotten, the wonders, the blessings, the miracles of that day. And God did it all openly, before all people.

When I left the county a few days later, I was thrilled that the work of my youth had not been wasted. How wonderful to see the growth which had taken place in the county over the years, in churches which I had planted twenty-five years earlier. And how wonderful to have my ministry affirmed in such a way.

God had shown that His power was too great to be contained. His Spirit moved out into the streets in an act of spontaneity. He is a God of liberty, always able to surprise us and do a new thing to show the world His love, His wonders, His goodness.

13 *Persecution*

Pull me out of the net that they have laid privily for me, for thou art my strength.

Psalm 31 verse 4

It seemed to be a pretty 'normal' day in our crusading programme across England. I had been twice before to Gloucester, a beautiful city, a very responsive community. I love the people there, they are open to Jesus and the Gospel. Not a sceptical, hard indifferent city, but a people who seem to be like the 'Bereans' mentioned in Acts – sincere, guileless and discerning of the sincere. The only thing about the city is the indifference in most of its churches, there is very little interest in the Christian communion in reaching out in evangelism. My organizers have tried again and again to interest them, but to no avail. By contrast the non-church public is eager to hear of Christ, flock to our meetings with packed services overflowing, numbers increasing every time we go.

I did not know what was about to break in the usually tranquil West Country city. We had had a crammed afternoon service, midweek, on a Wednesday. We had to turn people away, so many had arrived to get in. We gave reserved tickets for those unable to find a place for the evening meeting, guaranteeing them a seat as they were unable to gain admittance to the afternoon meeting. Many were healed, wheelchairs, sticks, neck braces all discarded. The wonderful power of God was manifested. Then after a rest at a friend's house in the City we were ready to start again at the evening meeting. The Community Centre was absolutely densely crowded, people still queuing to get in when we arrived for the gathering.

I saw that warm July evening the bright colours, young people in their tight jeans, lads in their white sweatshirts, older ladies, some in the sweltering heat still had hats on, there was chatter, expectation, some were being aided by relatives, some leaning heavily on sticks, stewards were lifting wheelchairs up the step, a blind man with dark glasses shuffled along nearer the door – the usual scene of anticipation, desperate need, people beginning to turn in hope towards God. . . . My heart mellowed as I looked forward to another successful night of deliverance by the power of prayer for these dear, precious needy ones. . . .

The service ran well. Roland Parsons and John Bryant were our leaders, the worship was beautiful, the 'anointing' fell so often down upon the service, this time well before I stood up to preach. I had great hopes of a night to remember. It was certainly to be that in more ways than one.

The press were present, but this is often the case in my meetings, so it was nothing new. John handed over to me, I read my text and began to preach. Reporters sat in their often normal stance, diffident till the time of the 'laying on of hands' begins, this is what always seems to interest them, what they often term the 'famous' moment when the 'miracles happen'. They sat solemnly having to 'put up with my sermon', till healing time began. Then I made a statement I quite regularly make in my sermons:

'The church must awaken, the enemy is at the gates. Our country is threatened by many counterfeit religions, many false prophets. . .they are fighting for the minds of the British people, as they seek to win men and women all over the world. We have the only message that can change human nature, Christ is the only Saviour, He is exclusive. Jesus said – 'I am the way, the truth and the life. . .no man cometh unto the Father [God] but by Me. . .' that is through Jesus the son of God. . .

Not through Mohammed, Buddha, BaHai, Confucius, Rev. Moon, Hari Krishna, or anyone else. Jesus is the only way. Islam is not the way. We do not need any false, foreign religions. We need only Christ Jesus, who is King, Lord, very God of very God.'

Suddenly, as I looked over my Bible, there was some shuffling on my right hand side near the platform. The two reporters and photographer were having a noisy, rather loud discussion. They suddenly stood, and approached the bottom of the platform steps, standing at my feet and looking up. I continued, not taking much notice:

'It is not by any religion, not through any man, minister, priest, elder, church, tradition *not even through an evangelist that we can be saved. . .only through Christ. There is only one mediator between God and man*, the man Christ Jesus. . .'

There was a flash of a camera. The two reporters were writing on their notepads like mad, and talking in subdued but audible sounds at my feet in full view of the people. Another flash, almost in my face; more chatter. I just kept going, wondering at the back of my mind what had set them off, half-pleased if they were writing my sermon down for a change and not only interested in the miracles. Usually, very little if any space was given to anything said in my sermon; but it seemed they were getting the message, I thought as I continued with the Gospel word. Soon I made my appeal. A great number responded and the counselling time went on for twenty minutes or so. Finally came the healing time.

Only one reporter was left by now. He spoke to a lady who had jumped from a wheelchair and others, evidently clearly healed. The long day closed with rejoicing, singing; so many going home at peace with their maker, happy, free, healed of pain, depression, their paralysed limbs free, crippled conditions relaxed, darkened eyes full of light and sight, little children

94

breathing free of asthmatic clogged lungs and so much more. . . . The reporters and photographers had gone. I thought they had seen all they had wanted and were convinced. I returned home exhausted.

The next day, early, a telephone call came from my local crusade organiser: 'I am inundated, Melvin, with questions from two reporters, about a statement you made last night about Islam being a false religion; about Jesus being the only way.' I agreed with my man in Gloucester: we could not backtrack on a fact we had mentioned amongst many other facts, including the statement I also had made that 'no evangelist or evangelical church can save anyone also. . .*only Jesus himself saves, forgives, gives certainty of eternal life. . .*'

My leaders in Gloucester, being just young men, delighted in a spiritual battle; especially, as they pointed out, all publicity and intense interest was upon the message we were preaching, howbeit one-sided, rather than the miracles of healing which were very rarely disputed. Now, for the first time, they were looking at our 2,000-year-old message, for which God had made us heralds, criers, announcers and proclaimers of Jesus Christ, God's Son, Saviour, Lord, Coming King, Crucified, dead, buried, but resurrected from the dead and coming Judge of our World. . . .

Soon more telephone calls came through. A leading reporter of a large West of England paper rang to ask what I had actually said. When I spelt out the same statement from my sermon, backed up with Holy Scripture, he gave a gasp:

'Do you know, this is dynamite Reverend Banks?'

The following day I received news of the first headlines: 'THE RACIALIST PREACHER'. Muslim leaders in the City said they would take it to the Race Relations Board as it was against the law! The battle began to rage.

The next week I was preaching in Cornwall, when BBC Radio rang me from London to enquire whether I would

95

go on their programme and defend what I had said. So from Cornwall I answered questions that touched a few million early the next Sunday morning. The questions went like this:

Question: Did you use the word Heathen? And in what context did you mean it?

My answer: I certainly did, we sent out missionaries to win the heathen, the Bible tells us to convert the heathen, it means 'those who worship other gods but the true God; who bow down to graven images, breaking one of the ten commandments (Exodus 20:4–5), which are binding on all the human race. We must love, help, show peace and lead to the joy of true Salvation those in this lost condition. . .whether they are black, white, European, Asian, African or any other race.'

Question: Did you call Islam a false religion?

Answer: I certainly did, Jesus said 'I am the way, the truth and the life, no man cometh unto the father but by me. . .'

Jesus is exclusive, Scripture says – 'There is none other name under heaven whereby we must be saved. . .but the name of Jesus'. Islam attacks Christianity, in its advertisements for its Albert Hall rallies recently it publicized – '*Christ Crucifixion or Crucifiction?*'

They are allowed to make blasphemous statements, while we are not allowed to point out simply the historic Christian message in this country that Jesus is Lord, true saviour, the only way to heaven, God and everlasting life. And this upsets people.

Question: Do you not think this a racialist statement?

Answer: Is it now racialist to defend the historic religion of nearly two thousand years in this country? I have not mentioned race, colour, language, ethnic culture. Only, *that Jesus is the world's only hope!*

Question: If Islam is a foreign religion, is not Christianity also? Did it not begin in the Middle East? Is not Israel a foreign country from the UK?

Answer: Jesus is not a foreign religion, he is a person. He did not come from Israel; He came from heaven. God is a spirit and those who worship him must worship not Mohammed or BaHai or Buddha but worship Christ in spirit and truth. Jesus said: 'He that hath seen me hath seen the father.' Jesus is beyond race, culture, no country can claim him. He belongs forever to all men. . .

Thus the interview drew near to its end. But what a witness!

The final question was: Will you not apologize, will you not withdraw your statement in your sermon?

Answer: How can I withdraw the Word of God? How can I step down from what the Bible declares, that Jesus is the only Saviour for Muslim, Buddhist, Confucius, Hindu, Roman Catholic or Protestant? . . .'

Now the time bomb which my remarks had set off *really* exploded. I was threatened with court action for violating the race relations law. I consulted my solicitor and told him that I would not pay any fines or agree to being 'bound over to keep the peace'. He thought this might lead to a one-month prison sentence, but also to great public sympathy and perhaps an early release by the Home Secretary. I was convinced that I should not compromise, and recalled George Eliot's words in *Janet's Repentance*:

Any coward can fight a battle when he's sure of winning, but give me the man who has pluck to fight when he's sure of losing. That's my way, Sir! And there are many victories worse than defeat.

In the tense, nerve-racking, exhausting days that followed, I found comfort and support in many things. I read an old sermon of the Scots Covenanters, which declared:

> Friend, all compromises tend to strengthen the Devil's hand, not the hand of the people of God. There is no discharge in this war. I have taken the sword, I have thrown away the scabbard. The only scabbard now for that sword is the hearts of the King's enemies. Let us use that sword with power today. Let us not be afraid of the battle.

Then I read the prophet Micah, and thoughts crowded in from God: I will weep and wail and go about barefoot and naked; howl like a jackal; moan like an owl – for her (the nation's) wound is incurable (Micah 1:8–9). And I compared his time with my own: abortion, child slaughter, homosexuality, stealing, crime, rape, broken homes, abused children, our prisons full of young men – the darkness is indeed very deep. Mosques, temples, two thousand Islamic prayer houses proliferating across the land, heathen religions and false religions springing up everywhere. . . . The prophet would have indeed cried out today had he been here.

Besides support; Micah also brought me comfort:

> Let us go up to the mountain of the Lord, and to the house of the God of Jacob; and he will teach us his ways and we will walk in his paths. . . . And he shall judge among many people, and rebuke strong nations afar off. . . . They shall sit, every man under his vine and under his fig tree; and none shall make them afraid.

> Micah 4:2–4

Support and comfort came, too, from many friends and fellow ministers. Jim Wilkinson of the Holly Bush

Fellowship called me, others also, from all parts of the nation; the General Secretary of my denomination, the Assemblies of God, rang to give his fullest support; Brian Hewitt of Redemption Magazine rang, too. I heard from many pastors, not just from Pentecostal churches but from non-charismatic fellowships, such as a Brethren group in Gloucester and a local Baptist minister.

But I had to hold on to the scripture: 'What time I am afraid I will trust thee.' For I learnt there were no great testimonies without tests. I was particularly hurt that many ministers in and outside Gloucester were strangely silent. Would that others had been too! The local archdeacon remarked that 'this sort of preaching from itinerant evangelists does not help local unity'. The mayor, who claimed to be Christian, distanced himself and said he opposed my message. Other Christians, too, were looking for my corpse to feed on. I felt strangely intimidated by the Evil One, and at one point was close to retracting. But my team steadied me and stood by, urging me not to back down to pressure, as this would deny the Gospel. Even if what I had said was misinterpreted, they argued, the truth of the Gospel would surface in the end.

So I pressed on, fighting back, quoting Scripture, defending the faith. The press had a field day. One newspaper devoted the whole of its editorial to attack me and my team. They said that there was no doubt about the amazing gift of healing that was given to me, but that with this gift, I had noble responsibilities. Great numbers hung on every word I said, it went on, and to abuse this position by attacking other religions and by being bigoted was to misuse my honorable position. 'If only he kept to healing, he would be untouchable', it said.

By this stage I fully expected to be the first Christian in the country to go to prison for his faith since John Bunyan. But I still held on, knowing I would be in good company: the Pentecostal preacher Nilstrom was imprisoned in Norway for calling homosexuality a sin; in Denmark, Dr Harriett had been struck off the medical register for standing out against abortion; in Sweden, another preacher, Ulk Ulkman, was sentenced and fined for telling his congregation to discipline their children, smacking them if necessary. If I was going to stand for Christ like these men, ought I not to be willing to be God's jailbird?

* * *

How did things finish?

An ITV producer rang me. Could I appear on a dinner-time programme? The chauffeur would arrive early the next morning:

'Things are coming to a head, and we want a debate with a representative of the Race Relations Board and another minister. This will be really hot, and it's going out live,' he announced. I had to go to Nottingham for the telecast. The chauffeur who drove me was evidently not a Christian but had heard and read all about the 'big' debate. He wished me luck as I left him at the car and walked through the TV headquarters' main entrance. I laughed and went on my way, not with luck but prayer in every breath!

The TV show was a resounding success. Later, the chauffeur, driving me home said:

'You dominated it. You sure had the answers for them. They never stood a chance Réverend Banks.' And then he added, thoughtfully. 'And you know, come to think of it, we have always been brought up to it even though I've never been very religious or gone to church since I was a boy. We were brought to believe in the good Lord above. Why should we change now? It was good enough for our parents, Grandpa and Ma; why should we turn to something we don't know anything about? Yes, Reverend, you're right: That Jesus is the right way. You got a point there, Sir. . .'. From the lips of a working-class unchurched man, a simple person; indeed, he summed it up: In Christ we have what we want and more. . .Jesus is the only way.

The day after, I had a telephone call: 'It's all over', one of my team said. 'I heard from one of the opposition, because of the strong public feeling and the likelihood that the court would throw it out. It had stirred up so much strong feelings on both sides of the fence. Any court case would be dropped this time.' I told Roland to make it known straight away in the press that in three weeks' time I would be speaking at a rally in the large school hall in Gloucester and that I would be repeating my statement again.

Three weeks later, four hundred people came to the school hall, but by then all had been diffused. The media realized that a battle had been won, Race Relations realized. We were adamant, the general public almost to a man had taken our side and were proud of our uncompromising stand for the truth of the Bible. I stood and, to a hushed audience, repeated the biblical fact:

'Jesus is the only hope and saviour of mankind, he is the saviour of the whole world. . .we need no other way, can turn to no other way, and if you have a great need for Christ', I said – 'there is a great Christ to meet your need. . . .' To cheers and prolonged clapping the story ended. One hundred people turned to Christ that day. And on our many visits to Gloucester, we are received by the largest possible crowds, with the greatest respect and love. In fact, I have more friends per population in that city, than in any other area of the world today.

The people of that West Country county will not forget the stand by God's help we were able to take. . . And its impact on hundreds of thousands of our fellow Britains.

A PS – I received a few weeks later a letter from a Muslim gentleman who told how he had never been to a Christian meeting in his life. Then he had attended my Service in Lancashire and been shown the greatest kindness and love he had ever discovered, had found Christ to be the Son of God, and had been totally healed of his pain, sickness and paralysed conditions. What a marvellous confirmation. . . . For in the end we are not called primarily to win mere legal, moral and theological battles only, *but first and foremost to capture and win men's and women's hearts with the love of God.*

PART TWO

Divine Wonders

14 Divine Wonders that have Touched a Nation's Heart

God. . .which doeth great things past finding out, yea, marvellous wonders without number.
Joel Chapter 9 verses 2 and 10

Many are the heart-warming stories that can be recounted from the years of my ministry, many stories of lives transformed completely and miraculously by the power of the Gospel. And even as this book is being published, those stories are being added to. I hold some sixty healing missions each year, which now touch as many as ten nations a year as I try to respond to invitations from the great revival areas around the world. At the same time I try to spend at least seven or eight months of each year in Britain. Even now I am planting churches, holding missions with Christian fellowships, prayer groups, churches and house meetings connected with all the major denominations and with none. I am still crusading in the largest public auditoriums and the biggest churches; but also in some of the smallest, too, where even in tiny villages and towns you have to reserve a seat or arrive hours early in order to get in, the crowds are so great.

So, as you see, it is not easy to pick out a few of the happy memories and real-life stories to whet your appetite and give glory to God. But here are some I want to share for now.

The hunchback of Macclesfield

It was in a big tent in Macclesfield. When we saw the hunchback's condition, our hearts were touched not only with compassion, but also with admiration. What faith! What a miracle would be needed, though, to cure such a lump. Yet, as we prayed, the crowd fell silent with speculation and wonder. Then came gasps, cries, tears and sobbing, as the coat fell limp where the tailor had built the material up to accommodate the hump. Soon the yard or so of extra material lay like an empty sack, flopping about on the man's back. The cheering did not abate for some minutes, and we all went home in wonder, fear, love and praise. No wonder a thousand people made a decision for Christ during those revival meetings.

The cured lady who complained

The lady who came back after a healing service in the Midlands had been so stone deaf she had not been able to hear a car revving up next to her. She had been cut off from the rest of the world by a wall of silence. One night I heard her loud voice complaining to the local pastor, big, jovial, blunt Geordie, Bob Smith. A minute later there came a knock at the door of the vestry, where I was deep in Bible study. Bob came in.

'We have a problem here, Melvin.'

'My whole ministry is made up of people's problems', I replied. 'What's new about this one?'

'Oh, this one's different. This lady [I peered around him and spotted her standing outside the door] this lady got healed the other night. She'd been stone deaf, never heard since her childhood sixty years ago. And now she can't sleep!'

'Why is that?', I asked, bewildered.

'Because she hears so well now, she is kept awake by the clock ticking in the bedroom *of the house next door.*'

You can't win, can you! (We suggested she moved her bed to the opposite wall of her room, or asked her neighbour to move his clock downstairs.)

Seeing after seventy years

One thrilling story relates to a Lancashire lady, who was touched during my Accrington healing mission two years ago. When ITV Granada talked to her, broadcast to a vast audience just after the main news, she was walking in her garden, talking to the interviewer, learning to appreciate the sights she could now see for the first time in her life. Through the laying on of hands and through prayer, God touched her, and slowly a lifetime of darkness slipped away.

I remember the night she was healed. As I prayed with our local Assemblies of God pastor beside me, she said she saw strips of light. I wondered for a moment what she meant, then realized that behind my back the street lamps were shining through the long strip windows of the church. This was how her sight began, and it grew in clarity over the months which followed. It was a true miracle, touching the hearts of the general public in the North of England.

The fish and chip shop incident

The meeting in the Birmingham suburb was crowded with reporters and photographers. As I moved down the long line of sick and incurable people, they followed me, pouncing on anyone who felt any sense of power, any feeling of improvement or pain receding or sight coming.

'Did you know Mr Banks before?' 'Have you ever met him?' 'Is this your first visit to a crusade?' 'How do you feel?' Thus it went on, and when a man walked the length of the church without his two sticks, this really got them going!

But then I came to someone in a wheelchair – a poor, pain-riddled, paralysed person. I spoke gently to her, and began to pray. But no response. No feeling of the power from God flowing through me and into her. It was like the sea in a storm dashing against a great quayside and splashing back again with no effect. I struggled, I sweated, I prayed with compassion and earnestness for a full ten minutes, but not a twinkle of feeling, no response, no healing, no life, nothing happening in her at all. The reporters hung on every prayer, but as I got weaker and more discouraged, they got more deflated. With a final word or two of love and faith, I tried to encourage her and then moved on to someone else.

The evening ended, and on the whole it had been a successful night. Most folk seemed to have been healed and even the reporters were thrilled. But as I drove to my digs in the city, I could not forget that one lady in the wheelchair. If only she had walked. . . .

The Bible says, the wind bloweth where it listeth: who can understand the mysterious movings of God? I felt a failure because of that dear lady not being healed, but God knew best.

At about the same time as I was driving home dejectedly, the lady's husband was lifting his wife into the front seat of their car as usual. They drove home, but on the way he stopped at a fish and chip shop to pick up some supper. When he returned to the car with the food, he found the car door open and his wife gone. What could have happened? Had she been kidnapped?

Then he looked up the street, and there, under a lamp, he saw her – walking by herself along the pavement towards their home! He had to lean against the car to steady himself. Then he jumped into the car to catch her up.

The next night she came back to the crusade to give her testimony – with no reporters present this time. She told how, as she sat in the car outside the shop, she had felt this mighty, loosening warmth spreading through her body. She felt the urge to try to move her legs and when she did so, she felt no pain. So she shuffled them a little, opened the car door and climbed out by herself. Almost immediately she could stand up and then *she felt she just wanted to walk home.* She felt so confident and strong. And she has remained well ever since.

The goal that was divine

He was a million-pound footballer, amongst the first. His name was famous, with headlines on sports pages of all the big dailies. He was raved over. But his knee and cartilege had been knocked out of place; his leg was in a very bad condition from a nasty clash in the midst of a vital match which had left him missing a good part of the rest of the season.

One of my meetings had been recommended to him in passing. He was not 'the religious sort' but needed to try anything! He came and was astonished (I heard later) by what he had witnessed in the service that night: sick people being healed, he could hardly believe his eyes. Then his turn came. He said he 'turned queer' as I prayed, as if under a dose of anaesthetic, although it was 'warm, sweet and a nice feeling'. . .an experience he had never ever 'touched before'.

To cut a long story short, he was playing the next Saturday, amazing physiotherapists, trainers and his manager and staff. *And* the sunday papers featured his terrific goal in that match. One paper in its headline on the sports page put it – 'that goal was just *divine*.' They did not know where he had been, or that it was true in more ways than one!

That famous player has never forgotten that prayer of faith which changed his life.

Last minute miracle

I was crusading in Blackpool in the North of England, the great seaside town, the 'Las Vegas' of Britain, the sin city of the North. I was warned by friends that this town was the 'evangelist's graveyard'. Many preachers had gone there and had given up in despair. I started that November night, but only a small crowd of about thirty people came, few were saved or healed, no miracles. . .all the week. It was a ten day mission, and by Saturday it was so poor, I realized I had 'met my Waterloo', that my friends were right. In spite of good advertising, much earnest prayer, fasting, this was just not moving. I said to an assistant:

'I will go home after the evening meeting Saturday, you finish the last four days of the mission'. I had given up. But, half-way through my sermon, the doors clattered and the small congregation of twenty-five to thirty people all turned round to see four people carry in a camp bed through the open doors, with a paralysed woman on it! I continued my sermon eyeing this poor, sick, young woman of about twenty-eight years of age. She was paralysed from the head down, she could hardly speak, not move and had to be spoon-fed!

After the end of the service, I went up to her before leaving for home after the hardest week of my life in crusading evangelistic ministry. As I laid hands on the pitiful young woman, immediately she arose with help crying:

'I can feel my feet'. True enough her feet began to move. After more prayer, encouragement, help, she could walk with the aid of two people, still weak but amazingly she could walk for the first time for three years. She went out to the car with help instead of being carried out! I decided to stay for another day or two, soon the audience doubled, and many more were saved and healed.

The largest national newspaper in England, read the next Sunday: 'woman carried into church on bed walks out'. Nearly half the nation read her story. I stayed on in the town for an extra week, nearly three weeks there. Crutches were cast away, sticks, wheelchairs discarded, five hundreds were saved. Two halls were packed, with a relay to another venue. On the last two nights there was an amazing awakening. It was not our Waterloo, *but God's great victory*. I have been back to Blackpool since for other good meetings, and we now have a booming, successful church there!

Famous opera singer gets a new song

Just before the service, after our prayer-time together with the elders and staff, I was told that one of Europe's most famous opera singers was present with us. She had flown from the Continent, to be in the service, having heard of the marvellous miracles in our services. She had lost her voice and had not been able to sing for a year, cancelling her engagements around the world. She is renowned in the international operatic world. Following the song service, worship, the preaching of the Word of God, a great long queue of sick people formed for the laying on of hands and prayer, as is customary in our meetings.

When the lady reached me, the lady stewardess and healing-line worker explained she could not speak or sing. I asked her to nod her head in answer to my questions. I asked her would she give her life to Jesus. The worker explained that the woman was a Roman Catholic but she agreed she had neglected religion and did not know Jesus as her Saviour. She agreed to come to Christ!

I asked her if she would sing regularly for Jesus now. She nodded. I prayed; she gulped, she spoke faintly: 'I can swallow properly, I can speak. I can speak', she shouted. I asked her to sing for Jesus *now*. She got a hymn book and sang beautifully and clearly, filling the auditorium with her rich voice *'the old rugged cross'*. . .

> 'On a hill far away, stood an old rugged cross
> The emblem of suffering and shame
> . . . .I will cling to the old rugged cross
> till my trophies at last I lay down. . .'

She is still singing for Jesus around the world and has not yet laid her trophies down in heaven. She was singing recently in the New York Opera House and also Covent Garden. But she sings for Jesus regularly in churches and functions in between.

God Gave Her a New Heart, a New Voice, a New Song to Sing to the World. . .

'I was going to put my head in the gas oven until that night my child was healed'

So said the tall dark twenty-five-year-old mother of a little brain-damaged child on Britain's West Coast. I had been holding a mission there, and we had dealt with hundreds of poor sick people for a week-long, fatiguing mission. This mother held the limp, weak, almost lifeless body in her arms tight across her chest.

'There is no hope unless he gets a miracle today. We need a miracle', she sobbed. The child, if it lived long enough I was told, would never sit up, never communicate, never recognize anyone!

I prayed. The father stood halfway up the crowded aisle, watching, half-unsure, feeling forlorn and helpless. I prayed on a *strong prayer*. . .the mother wept louder, a lady worker put her arm around her. I went on praying down the line. About fifteen minutes later there was near hysteria in one corner, shouting, laughing, clapping. I gazed over and we heard the child had opened its eyes and was looking around, seemingly trying to communicate.

I was back in that area one year later, and little Chris was walking, running up and down the aisle of the church, now begging to say some words, communicating, healthy, noisy, strong; the child the best surgeons, specialists and doctors said would not live and if he lived he would not sit up, would be a cabbage in its short life here – that little fellow certainly shot up enough steam in that service to make everyone know he was very much *alive. . .and would be for a long time to come*. Faithful Christians know that family follows the Master who is the great miracle worker today – Jesus Christ of Nazareth!

'I must leave my lover and go home to my child and husband'

These were the words of a young woman in the counselling area, following a night of revival in South Shields on the North–East coast of Britain. I had preached the Gospel to the packed chapel and made my customary appeal, that sacred moment when we ask people who feel deeply convicted in their hearts, who are willing to repent (to turn away from their sins with sorrow) and commit themselves to Jesus Christ, to make Him their Saviour and Lord, to ask him to come and save them although unworthy. Many came. The whole front of the chapel altar and around the pulpit was filled.

Some fifteen miles away in Co. Durham a little boy was being put to bed. He knelt to say his prayers, his Father – apprehensive and doubtful – let him pray. The six-year-old prayed:

'Lord, send Mum home tomorrow, you can do it God, please talk to Mummy tonight and tell her to come home tomorrow, Amen!'

His Dad tucked him into bed and said, 'Goodnight Son'. Hiding a tear, the little fellow said perkily: 'Good-

113

night Dad, don't worry. Mum will be home tomorrow because I asked God!!' The father slipped out of the room not knowing what to say!

Meanwhile, two and a half hours later, as I made that appeal in South Shields, among those who came forward was *that mother*. She had left her husband, home and little boy for a lover, months before. Now drawn by the Crusade she was weeping before God. All came out as she shared it with two of my team ten minutes later. She found God to be real, forgiveness that was certain, and the Holy Spirit to be her purifier.

Soon she made that confession, and we heard later she had packed her bags, left the man she was living with *and the next day returned home to her husband and child*. They are happily married today and living wholesome, clean lives. What *special joy* I find in seeing this happen *often – the miracle of a restored, reconciled family* – One of life's *greatest miracles*!

£10,000 stolen money returned

The minister ushered the small but well-built lady into the vestry. I never see ladies alone for counselling, but had made an allowance on this one occasion due to the requests of the pastor. The meeting was just over, we had seen every miracle in the book in this small Welsh town. The place had been packed so much I thought folk were going to faint. No doubt the blind woman who had received her sight a few days before and had been featured in the paper that night had even further expanded the already congested conditions. I was really thinking of these practical problems, of how we could manage when no hall was available to us in the town, when the little lady began with a soft Welsh voice:

'Thank you for seeing me, Reverend Banks, I do have a great problem. . .' I had heard it all before, but everyone thinks they are the only people who have done such

114

wrong, made such mistakes or lowered themselves in such a way, so I let her go on.

'It's like this, I have had such a responsible position on the firm. . .' She told me how she had been a trusted employee for many decades, handling large sums of cash. She had finally fallen to temptation, though it would be almost impossible for the firm to find out how much and what had been stolen. £10,000 had been involved (that would be worth more like £100,000 today!) She could not be caught out.

But in my meeting that night her conscience had been so awakened and pricked and wounded that she could never find peace until this had been sorted out. She felt terrible. The Holy Spirit had done his work, the spirit of honesty and power; and fear of God had moved her spirit for good. It was quite clear God had done something very direct and deep in her heart, for she had no ulterior motive and was quite beyond any police action.

Her whole story convinced and stunned me. God had ministered a very heavy conviction of sin and clearly pointed her to the need of restitution, as Zacchaeus had done in Luke 19:8 when he repaid back all he stole and four times as much. I administered both comfort and peace, and followed on with the efforts to urge her to follow this conviction through. I gave her the assurance the church would stand by her, believers would secretly pray, and if it meant prison they would visit her. No shame would stand in the way of us showing loving kindness, helpfulness to her family, and being true friends, brothers and sisters all the way.

She left that vestry at peace. Later she was to see God answer prayer with mercy shown by the employers. She paid back all she stole; she was not taken to court or sacked. She lost some wages in that she was demoted to a lower position in the firm, but she still works there, is admired by her bosses, is a born again believer of good and fine character and a great witness to this day for Jesus to the world.

Simon's miracle shakes Suburbia

Derek was a pastor's son, brought up by a faithful, hard-working, devoted, Assemblies of God pastor in the suburban town of Reading. Hard sophisticated areas not known for their over-religious intensity, the London suburbia towns are often moved by church activity. The rat race of materialism causes their large populations to be rushing from Monday to Saturday, living hard, working all hours to keep up their high life style, and Sunday is the one day to play golf, go fishing, take a drive, or sleep in all the morning, or if particularly sinful, do your Sunday shopping. But Ernie and Emily his wife never gave up for thirty years. I have never known a more dedicated couple. But while one son was associate pastor and choir leader, the other, Derek, brought sadness to their hearts. He had done well in his own business and had made it in life, he lived well, a month's holiday a year in foreign parts, the best, largest of cars, fully computerised office, well before it was hardly known how to use computers, and a lovely house. He had done well in life, and had a lovely wife and a young son called Simon.

I was sitting in Pastor Appleby's house the last day of the successful crusade, which had included the healing of a boy who had been told by the Reading Royal Berkshire Hospital that he would never walk, but would permanently have to pull himself round on his tummy, since there were no nerves in his legs at all. This boy was now beginning to stand and walk; within three weeks of the mission he could run around. The miracle hit the headlines in large papers and was read by hundreds of thousands of non-church folk. God had blessed this, my second visit to Reading.

116

But as we sat chatting over tea, just before going to the evening meeting, the front door opened and someone crept along the passage outside where we sat. I commented: 'Someone has just come in. Is that a burglar?'

'No', Pastor Appleby replied, 'unless you call my second son a burglar.' With a smile, he went on: 'Derek doesn't like to meet preachers. If he can keep out of their way he will. . .'

I moved towards the living room door, just to catch him heading back down the passage to slip away unnoticed if possible.

'Hello Derek', I called. He turned, red-faced, as he held on to the front door know – 'Hello. . . . I have to go', he added nervously. He made a brief, courteous comment and was gone.

There is a man who is running from the Lord, I thought. I stood and quietly while Ernie and his wife were clearing away the tea cups and washing up, I followed in a beeline out to his car. I prayed for him all the way even as he turned his car round in seconds and drove off fast, at great speed. I prayed: '*he will need a miracle to restore him, conquer his heart. . .bring him face to face with you Lord. . .give him a miracle, save him, his wife and child. . .*you know how faithful Pastor Appleby has been, now answer my prayer soon. . . O Lord Jesus. . .'

One day, months later, a telephone call came from Ernie:

'Can you come next year and give me some more meetings, Melvin? It will be eighteen months since the revival blessing we had here and the Lord is really moving in our Church.'

I looked at my desk diary that was so full for the year ahead, then agreed on a date about fifteen months ahead. Then Ernie added: 'By the way, your prayers for my son Derek, do you remember?' I thought for a moment, but of course I did, and the son and Mrs Appleby junior.

'Well, we had a lot of distress just recently. Not long after you had gone, the big London children's hospital told us Simon was going to die. They could not operate, he had a tumour the size of a cricket ball next to the stomach! He was only five years of age, and to lose their only child, what despair I thought.

But prayer had been answered, Ernie told me! Derek suddenly, after years of indifference, apathy, hardness, wept and sought God. He came to Jesus, Anne, his wife, repented and was born again also, the whole church joined in fasting. But the prayer that set it off happened months before any of this was known. This was the start of a line of blessing that was to bring an outstanding miracle to a dying child and be a witness to a deathly spiritual community, and to show Jesus was alive! It was to bring a family to Christ and a mini-revival to this Assemblies of God church – Mount Zion, Earley, Reading. Amazing. . .

Within a few months the hospital (Derek had refused all medical aid and medicines and drugs for Simon) cleared him, a 'marvellous' cure. He was healed, saved and today, nearly 13 years later, he is a teenager, plays the organ brilliantly, belongs to the church, serves the Lord with his parents (Derek is now a Deacon of Mount Zion). . . and never has had any relapse or sign of the tumour since. *He was saved from death. A miracle that shook an indifferent society, showing the love and goodness and mercy of God.*

Helping to heal the after effects of the miners' strike

The big strike that lasted for twelve months, paralysing much of the coalfields of Britain, brought much bitterness between the mining people and much of the rest of the working people in Britain. Yorkshire people especially suffered in an unimaginable degree. In mining communities many villages drew closer together then ever before. Many normally peaceable, decent people were drawn into

118

an often vicious dispute, ending in confrontations, riots, violence, destruction, with even good people admitting they had done things, or behaved in ways they never dreamed they would have done prior to this struggle. Homes broke up, wives could stand it no longer and left their husbands; some committed suicide; six miners died; many were injured in scraps, often with the police; many families and communities were near starvation. When the strike came to an end in March 1985, I was invited to go for a three day mission centred at Grimethorpe in the heart of the Yorkshire coalfields. Around the village there had been much suffering, also many disputes and trouble with the police during the year-long strike. Whole communities in this area near to Barnsley relied almost entirely on coal for their source of employment.

Some friends told me I was brave to enter such an area where there had been so much bitterness. I felt no inclination to cancel. These were people who needed God's help, and coming only weeks after the strike had ended, seeing there would be many terrible scars, perhaps I could bring some healing through the Gospel and our Saviour to men's and women's hearts. Also some encouragement where there was much guilt and where people felt ashamed to belong to an area scorned by much of the rest of the nation as 'gangsters', 'animals', 'thick heads' and 'layabouts'. I never thought this, though. I knew or felt there were many fine people caught in a trap not of their own making, who wanted only peace and to care for their families and to work and live a happy life.

When I arrived, this is exactly what I found. Marvellous people. There was great interest, even many more of the 'curious' than normal, turning up at the meetings to hear 'this Southerner who dared enter the South Yorkshire Republic' as it is sometimes called. The meetings in the main community centre hall were packed, standing room only. I put people at ease, I spoke of Christ, refused to enter into politics, pointed them to the one who could heal their guilt-dilemma. Many were marvellously healed. One mother told me of the miraculous healing of her little baby with an incurable disease. When I entered the village again (six months later) she told me the hospital had cleared the baby after its wonderful healing, where there had been no hope.

Miracles, love, a Gospel that works, the healing words of Scripture can mend a community no matter what difficulties have torn it apart. Thank God for the healing Gospel! I believe that mission played some part, with the faithful ongoing work of the local pastors and Christians in bringing peace, eliminating bitterness in so many homes and lives after this devastating event.

The fire falls and the debt vanishes!

'I do want you to come to my town', Ben, the Scottish minister declared. He was pastor to a rising church in the Lincolnshire fen country. 'But to tell you the truth, the debt on our new building is so huge it will take us years to pay it off and to be able to afford any major evangelistic effort.'

'I believe God has spoken to me about moving this great country area, and market town', I declared. 'God can help us with all the money we need. I am sure about that.' Ben looked at me:

'Well, the church is looking up, excited with the new building. But we lack new life coming in: we lie on this huge council estate, and no one attends from the local area', he added. 'We must do something. . .but its that debt, if only we did not have that debt. . .', he murmured thoughtfully.

'Let's believe that the money will come in from the offerings for all advertising,' I added. 'Let us put people first, and their needs; that has always been my motto.' 'God cannot let us down. I will sell my little car and give you the money if necessary.' Ben looked up amazed:

'Now, I don't think we expect that', he said, a little embarrassed. 'Somehow we will find a little cash for the advertising, and then believe God for the rest through the offerings!' So we shook hands and what, unknown to us, was to become an historic event, was set in motion. . . .

In that crusade a chauffeur to the Royal family was converted; a paralysed girl ran from her wheelchair and was featured on the front page of the local newspaper, hundreds came to Christ. The crusade was extended and every inch of the building became congested with the crowds. The vast working-class housing estate, normally seeing few ever attending any church, saw many whole families converted to Christ, and the church became a centre for family worship for years afterwards.

Five hundred registered a commitment for Jesus during those days of power and blessing. Today there are two thriving Full Gospel churches in the town. Much has happened over the years, but God has worked and developed believers into two fellowships that are making separate but distinct impacts on the area.

But the notable *after-thought of God*, when he had worked so many miracles of regeneration and healing on this Lincolnshire town, was that not only were all financial needs met for the existing bills (the advertising of the crusade, heating, lighting of the church, etc.) but he added on a remarkable bonus! A telephone call came from the pastor to my office some weeks after the crusade had ended, thanking me and full of appreciation for the many new people crowding into his church now, and the marvellous testimonies of changed lives. And then he added:

'By the way, a strange thing has happened. Some gifts came this week from new friends of the church and this has cleared every penny of the huge debt. Instead of being saddled with this for twenty-five years, we have it cleared completely. It is amazing! I don't know how to say thank you. . .when. . .*the fire fell on this*

121

church, the debt vanished. . .it's miraculous. . .*put God first, put souls and people first*, like you said, make the sacrifice. . .*the Lord certainly takes care of everything else*.!'

No mention had been made of this debt; the general public did not know about it – no appeals, no requests, no fund-raising – nothing was done. It was purely the supernatural outcome of the Holy Spirit's blessing.

* * *

The following testimonies are some of the many that arrive in our postbag.

A minister's wife raised from her deathbed

'Over a decade ago I had meningitis. I had got a bit better but was very thin and weak but I knew something was wrong inside, that I was not as I should be. Eventually I was diagnosed as having ESR blood cancer, very serious – a 30 count – very poor, it was critical. I was a minister's wife, it did not worry me about dying but I did not want to leave my husband and two children who were still very small yet! I wanted to be alive for them.

'I asked the hospital if they would release me to go over the ferry from the Isle of Wight, where we lived at that time, to the Melvin Banks crusade in Portsmouth. I had to be carried onto the boat, I was so weak, I felt that I was dying and wondered whether I would make it to the meeting.

'I knew God could heal me, I was unconscious most of the journey on the ferry boat across to the mainland and did not come to until in the auditorium in the city of Portsmouth. The meeting was packed out, I could hardly cope, all these people, I just wilted in my heart. There was this little man buzzing about, I asked who it was, they said that's the evangelist Melvin Banks. I had heard about him and the marvellous gift of healing but he looked so ordinary, moving amongst the people, mixing, just like anyone else. . . It was so noisy, I felt only God could help me. . .the meeting was so long, I got down to the front, I thought, 'after all this effort and I feel so ill I am going to make an effort to get something from God.' A lady near me said, 'I am going for a blessing to get my corns healed.' I thought, if an old lady can believe for a few corns to go, what can He do for me if I trust Him through His servant. . .

'Then just in front of me was this poor little lady: she was so crippled, so bad and sick, my heart went out to her. I forgot myself. Melvin called her out. . .so wonderful, just amazing. . .she was so sick then in moments her body straightened before our eyes, her sickness vanished, her limbs became upright, all pain and suffering vanished. Then Melvin asked me what was wrong. . .I couldn't speak and tell him what was wrong with me, I was choked with emotion. Then what the Bible calls the gift of the Word of Knowledge came to him, he said, 'It's in your chest, isn't it?' I nodded, agreeing. He asked me to breathe in deeply, but I just felt I couldn't. It was difficult to get breath enough to keep alive. . . Yet alone to breath and breath as Melvin suggested, the pain was terrible. I tried, I made every effort; I thought it would kill me, but as I did so I felt amazing, thrilling me through and through: it was easing. I can only describe it like ten pints of new blood and ten times more fresh, new energy pumped into me! The power, the relief, the joy, the healing, the hope I received was marvellous. I went out of that great auditorium feeling as if I had never had anything ever wrong with me. It was gone midnight when we eventually got back across the water to the Isle of Wight and home. The next day I knew I was cured, no one had to lift me, help me, carry me any more. I had energy out of this world. I praised God like I had never done before. . .

'On Monday morning I was back at hospital, and it was unbelievable the response of the hospital staff. They treated me like a china doll first of all, of course, before all the tests started. I said, to their surprise (and possibly hidden amusement): 'I want to tell you – God has done something!'

'Do not worry, we know you are not quite yourself, you are poorly', they said, trying to excuse my state of mind.

'I am not poorly', I remonstrate with them. 'I am sane, I know what has happened to me. I'm well', I insisted. The test that glorious morning soon showed the blood count to be *now normal*! New flesh and blood had been created in my body.

'Schoolteachers are very logical people and I am no different. I am an enquiring sort of person as well as being a schoolteacher, and all my investigations, my long healthy years since have proved an outstanding miracle that cannot be explained in any other way. I have gone back to teaching, I have five children of my own now as well and a classful of forty kids! I'm a busy minister's wife, *fit and healthy ten years after that miracle and resurrection from death's doorway to new health, new life, new fullness. . .'*

Multiple sclerosis builds a church

'I had not been to church for forty years and only due to my wife's badgering and persuasion did I go along reluctantly to hear Melvin Banks when he came to the Community Centre, Clevedon, Somerset. I had sung in the choir as a boy but had had a row with the vicar and left in a temper and never went back to church except on my wedding day and the occasional funeral. I contracted multiple sclerosis some years ago and had a job getting about. My daughter and wife tried hard to get me to go and I turned up and stood by the door, leaning against the wall. I thought it was all madness and imagination.

'As the very lively service went along I was even more convinced they were all mad. People clapped, actually looked happy in church, they danced, joined hands, sang so loud I couldn't even hear my own voice. I was surprised at all the young people there. The service went on for a long time. I had spent five years with excruciating pain, diabetes for twenty years, multiple sclerosis. Drained and pained, sick and depressed I was just heading for the door when Reverend Banks called out to me. He said God could heal me. I responded, when asked if I believe that, I had my doubts but he went on to say Jesus loved me and wanted to reveal His power to me. He prayed and I felt such power through my body that I could not stand. It was the happiest feeling in my life; I felt *born again*. My pain just drained away, never to feel it any more from that day nearly seven years ago. No more MS, diabetes, pain, sickness, suffering.

'*It works. It's not old theology. It is practical, real, lasting, wonderful.* I am healthy, fit, I do my work as a gardener around Clevedon, everyone *knows that I am a walking miracle.* From that time a local new Family Church was established and has grown over the years, led by our fine outstanding local pastor. My miracles and others of MS and other sicknesses and the many conversions over the years through mighty signs and wonders in this town have built a fine church, now with a brand new building. It meets the needs of many people in this seaside community in the West of England. Just like in Bible days, miracles bring glory to God and help to build the Church, and show the power of the Kingdom of God and of our lovely Saviour Jesus Christ today.'

* * *

And in brief:-

Coronial arterial disease, then cured discharged by the Swansea Hospital

'I was under both Cardiff and the Swansea hospitals; told my arteries were badly diseased; I was cold all day long; very little blood getting through the blocked arteries. I was desperate. I saw in the paper Reverend Banks coming to Gorseinon. I felt a glow go through my body; pain continued, but all night I felt this glowing heat working through my body. I have been wonderful, the doctors are amazed, have cleared me, discharged me, they have reported my arteries were all wide open and clear of all disease. *"This"*, they said, *"was a miraculous healing"*.'

A Swansea Mother

Doctor said child would never sit up. . .–

'When I brought Craig to Reverend Banks' service in Swansea, he was in a pitiful state. I was a sad person; the doctors gave no hope either. Mr Banks prayed hard for him with great feeling and love. Today, eighteen months later, he is a miracle, running about, full of life – *what a change! what a miracle*! I am now a believer, and have been baptised.'
A Bridgend Mother
– So Thankful!

Girl had not walked for three years. . .–

Dear Reverend Banks,

I am writing to you from the bottom of my heart. I came to your meeting in Lyneham in March 1988. My daughter Margaret had been unable to walk for three years without a frame. . . . After your prayers, she gets stronger daily, and now walks alone, something my husband and I never thought we would see again. . . . She is so happy now. I felt a different person when I came away from your wonderful meeting.

Yours sincerely
Mrs E. H. Daunts
(North Wilts)

Leukemia healed

Dear Sir,

I would like to thank you for your prayers for my grandson Ryan, at Ebenezer Chapel. In June last year he was desperately ill with leukemia. The hospital warned us nothing could be done. . .deterioration continued. . . they decided to take him back to Ladywood Children's Cancer Hospital, Birmingham. His last blood test after your prayer suddenly showed it was substantially up. . .a week later that of a normal child. . . As he is today, ruddy cheeks, I am so grateful, thank you God.

Yours sincerely
Mrs J. M. Fulman

Cancer of the face disappears

This miracle changed my life completely, this rodent ulcer cancer on the side of my nose was healed, after prayer in Reverend Melvin Banks' mission to Great Yarmouth and Gorleston in 1984. It was gradual from that time, but it was completely healed. Also, all my depression of years evaporated after I gave my life to Jesus, which has filled my being with such joy and

purpose these past three and a half years as I have
learned to serve him.

Mrs Gibbs
Great Yarmouth, Norfolk

A witch is delivered

I was campaigning on the Eastern seaboard of England
at a small Norfolk fishing port. God was giving us the
greatest revival seen in the port since the great 1929
'fisherman's' revival under the tough, rough fisherman's
evangelist, Jock Troup. People queued up to get in.

The local vicar was in opposition.

'If I preached what that fellow preached, I would
empty my church', he said. Well, it *was filling ours*.
What a sad comment for someone to make who never
even came to hear *what I was preaching*. If the finished
work of Calvary, the Blood of Jesus, Repentance, Faith,
Justification, the Cross and Resurrection of Jesus would
empty a church, then better to empty it than preach any
other Gospel – I sent a message back to the Vicar and told
him – there was no reply! But the Bible says:

'*If I am lifted up from the earth (on the Cross) I will
draw all men unto me. . .*' It says this message would
draw men and women. I certainly never lack a crowd all
over Britain, and here on the Norfolk coast once again
people jammed into the meetings. But in the midst of
curious interest, and a few critics at the end of one night
I was approached by my chief counsellor, in charge of the
staff who talk to those who seek personal advice, enquire
about spiritual matters, etc. He said:

'Tonight do you know who got converted? A witch!'
I looked agog at him. The next night he pointed her out
to me, tall, slim, dressed in black, with many occult
trinkets around her neck and wrists. I saw the darkness
surrounding her face. She asked for more counsel and

advice again that night and each night; she came for longer talks with our most experienced advisors and helpers; more prayer for deliverance.

I will never forget the final great meeting as hundreds lifted their hands praising the *King of kings, Jesus,* singing –

'Majesty, worship His Majesty
Unto *him* be Glory, Honour and Praise'

and I noticed the ex-witch, with hands raised, radiant face, no dark clothes on now, no occult bangles, in bright colourful clothing, fresh, smiling. Light shone in her face. *O what power there is in the precious name of our lord to deliver even witches, devil worshippers and satanists through the mighty power and grace of the love of god in Christ, Jesus our lord!*

The vision

It was the end of a service where every wheelchair had been emptied as people walked, ran, leapt in the power of God – a remarkable meeting that stirred the crowded congregation of some hundreds of simple folk.

I was beckoned to the back of the hall, as I was about to head for my car and drive to my digs, somewhat exhausted after a heavy demanding evening. The elder of a local Christian Fellowship looked radiant and gasping, as if he had just been offered £5,000 for his birthday!

'Listen to this, Melvin', he said, introducing a well-dressed lady, speaking in a refined and educated voice. She told me about her daughter, pointing to her, about nine years of age, dressed in the uniform of what was clearly a private school.

'Maria is not given to telling stories, seeing things, exaggerating. She has no story-telling imagination, she has never been in one of these types of events before', the

129

mother related. 'I am astonished at what she keeps telling me she *saw* in the service tonight. . .' She gulped nervously, blushed a little. Then slowly she continued: 'She said, and she described so clearly to me. . .and being such a serious girl I don't doubt at all what she has told me. . .although for a while it took me some difficulty to accept. . .'

I looked at her, waiting with expectancy. It was possibly some minor diversion, some small experience, perhaps the wonder of the service for the first time, or the miracles had struck off a chord, I thought. Then it came. . .

'She told me about the tall, fair, white-haired man she had seen on the stage behind you, Mr Banks. He stood directly behind you all through the service. He was a marvellous-looking figure and very tall. . .she described everything about him. . . She thought first of all everyone could see him, but when I pointed out there was no one behind you but the curtains pulled, she just went on to tell me about him. . .' Either an angelic being had been amongst us, or even the third man – *our lord himself*. . . That little girl has never forgotten that experience and many years later still repeats her story unchanged!

A pub is converted!

It was in the same marvellous meeting that I was introduced to one of the sixty converts that night! The chief counselling steward introduced me to a tall thin lady:

'I have a problem.' I was so used to nearly everyone I met saying that, it did not take me aback. I only had to guess what it was, a family problem, cash problem, sickness problem, a son or daughter problem, or a scores of other needs that people share with me. No, this was to be different to anything I had ever heard before. . .

'I own a Pub.' It was me who was aghast now. 'It is a good hostelry; we have nice customers, a good business.

My husband died some years ago and I run it myself. But I do not know what to do now I have received Christ. What do you advise?'

I looked at her, thrilled with the grace of God to reach down to this needy lady. And yet, she was human like anyone else, was she not?

'Pray every day. A new world of guidance will open to you, your conscience will work, God will speak to you. You will know what to do.'

I never saw that lady till six months later. I was speaking at a crowded meeting in a school hall near Bodmin, North Cornwall; she had travelled some miles to be with us. She told me afterwards she had brought five people with her, some of her customers. She had put up Bible texts and also crusade posters about my meetings all around the pub; more of her customers were due to attend the next night. They now nicknamed her 'the preacher'. She had much opposition, but had been able to help a lot of her 'congregation'. She had prayed for folk and even led people to Jesus in the pub. It was getting a nickname of 'the soul-saving centre'. But opposition was mounting, plus the long hours she had to work, which was a hindrance to her getting Christian fellowship.

I saw her two years later while preaching near St Austell. She had by then sold her pub and was running a little shop near the seaside, going on and growing with God and still telling others of the miracle Christian. . .and still winning the lost. But in that area of north Cornwall, the pub is still known as the 'soul saving centre. . . !'

First World War soldier healed

I was in the crowded little village hall of Burgh-le-Marsh, near Skegness. The ancient church clock heralded the Gospel, as it boomed out each hour, with the text around the clock face: 'it is time to seek the Lord.' Unfortunately, the locals of this rural community had seen it so many thousands of times they accepted it as 'mundane' and 'old fashioned'. But we gave the village the chance of hearing the Gospel and seeking the Lord.

The hall was so crowded, many of the old windows were nailed or fastened, so we could not open them, it was a May evening and was an early summer, very warm and stiflingly hot in the building. Amongst the many I prayed for and led to Jesus was an elderly gentleman, helped in by a younger lady whom he introduced as his nurse. . .

A week later, a letter from the old gentleman arrived:

Dear Pastor Banks,
   Since the Battle of the Somme in 1916, when I received a nasty leg-wound through shrapnel, it has had to be bandaged twice a week by the nurse. But what a miracle when the nurse unbandaged the wound the next day: not a sign of the mark, even where the shrapnel had torn; in *fact no wound at all after sixty years*. . .I certainly believe in miracles . . .I cannot thank you enough. . .and above all the Almighty. . .

That dear old soldier continued to write to me, possibly for nearly ten years afterwards, till God took him to heaven. He died without a mark on his leg.

* * *

The last two stories came from newspaper reports:

Back in the swing again

Blind, deaf and crippled with arthritis, Mrs Violet Dixon plans to get back in the swing of things now she can see, hear, and walk again after meeting divine healer Melvin Banks when he visited Portsmouth.

Mrs Dixon (57) has thrown away the dark glasses she always used to wear, and put away the frame she needed to help her walk, after meeting Mr Banks at the Wesley Central Hall, Fratton.

Mrs Dixon who has been deaf for almost twelve years, lost her sight through shock almost four years ago after she was attacked and tied up outside her caravan home.

Today Mrs Dixon said: 'There is no way to describe how I feel. I can see, hear and walk much better now.'

Mrs Dixon told *The News* that Mr Banks, a minister in the Assembly of God, laid his hands on her head and forehead to cure her blindness, on her ears to cure her deafness and on her spine to cure her arthritis.

'He seemed to push my ears and then let go – it was like having a loudspeaker inside my head – I could hear so well.

'My sight gradually came back within three to four minutes and it seems to be getting much better. I cannot read print but Mr Banks said that will come with time.

'The arthritis that I had was so bad that I used to have to crawl and I cried with the pain.

'I am not a religious person – I hardly ever go to church – but I went to the meeting just in case there was any chance that I might be cured.

'I had no faith in God but as soon as I entered the hall my worries seemed to melt away', Mrs Dixon said.

Her husband, Stuart, said: 'I cannot deny that my wife is 100 per cent better.'

Neighbours in homes set aside for disabled people in Gatcombe Park, Hilsea, could hardly believe their eyes when they saw Mrs Dixon out walking her dog, Skippy.

The white-haired lady they knew was always huddled over a walking frame and always wore dark glasses.

Warden Mrs Jeanne Fernie was amazed when she met Mrs Dixon.

Only two weeks ago Mrs Fernie was called to Mrs Dixon's home where she lives with her husband, her dog, her cat and Peter the parrot, because she had fallen down and knocked herself out.

Ophthalmic surgeon, Mr Norman Ashworth, who

treats Mrs Dixon at the eye unit of Queen Alexandra Hospital, Cosham, said he was very surprised that she could see.

* * *

The other story comes from South Wales. Mrs Jennings said – '*I thought all he wanted was money – but I left my wheelchair behind*'

'Invalid Jessie claims blessing cured her'

Britain's best-known healing Evangelist makes a return visit to Swansea next week – and at least three women will make sure they are there to meet him.

Because the last time the Reverend Melvin Banks held prayer services in South West Wales, Mrs Miriam Ann Grassi, Mrs Jessie Jenkins and Mrs Ann Jones went to him for help. And each says that after their meetings they were healed in one way or another.

Next week Mr Banks will be at the Miracle Tabernacle Assemblies of God Church in West Street, Gorseinon. He was there, and at the Parish Hall in Llanelli, earlier this year when he attracted huge congregations.

Mr Banks is considered Britain's best-known healing Evangelist. His work has taken him to France, Germany, Austria, New Zealand and South Africa, as well as appearing on ITV and BBC radio.

'I am not the healer', he says. 'Jesus is the Saviour and the healer. I believe that these meetings will result in countless numbers finding faith in God and healing.'

And three women from Swansea, Burry Port and Neath would agree with those sentiments. None of them had been to the Gorseinon church or met Mr Banks before his last visit but now they are eager to meet him on his next.

Mrs Miriam Ann Grassi, aged forty-nine, went to see

134

him after reading about his healing in the *Evening Post*.

'I was very ill with heart disease' she said. 'My brother had died from it when he was thirty-two and my father when he was thirty-four. I used to work with the handicapped but I had to give the job up. I went to see Mr Banks and during the meeting he put his hands on me and prayed.

'For seven days after I went home I felt excruciating pain followed by a terrific healing heat of power. On the sixth day I went to Morriston Hospital for tests and they told me the coronary arteries were open. My doctor still keeps an eye on me now but I'm fit and well; I might even look for another job.'

Another grateful woman is Mrs Jessie Jennings, a 74-year-old from Burry Port. She saw Mr Banks on his visit to Llanelli and will be travelling to meet him again in Gorseinon next week.

She had been virtually confined to a wheelchair for twelve years and when she did walk, she needed two sticks for support. She also suffered from osteo- and rheumatoid-arthritis, could only barely move her hand and had severe pains in her back. But all that changed, she said, after meeting Mr Banks. 'My knees are still bad but the rest of my body is marvellous', she said. 'My back has been cured and I can even bend down to touch my toes. I can get in and out of bed without help now, and I only need one stick to walk. It's wonderful not being in pain all the time any more.

'I went to see him because my daughter Mavis nagged me to. I was utterly convinced he was a charlatan, but now I believe a miracle really did happen.'

And a final testimony came from Mrs Ann Jones of Miny-Coed in Cimla, Neath. Mrs Jones, aged thirty-eight, injured her neck and suffered from arthritis in both arms. The combined effect, she said, was that her legs were affected and she suffered from pains in her head, neck and upper half of her back.

She was forced to give up her work a year ago but has now found another job at Neath College. 'When Mr Banks put his hand on me and blessed me, I felt a tremendous heat, a burning going through me. Over the next few days I felt a tremendous difference and I'm fine again now.

'I am convinced that if I hadn't gone to the church on that day I would be an invalid by now.'

15 *How can We Work Miracles?*

> *If there be any excellence. . .set your mind on these things*
> Philippians Chapter 4 verse 48

I am often asked, 'How can one heal the sick?' 'Is there a key?' 'Does it work for everybody?' How can anyone get to say what the missionary Hudson Taylor said: 'First, it's impossible; secondly, it's difficult; and then thirdly, it's done!'

In my view, the problem is not so much *getting* God's power to do great things – the problem is *keeping* it. The reason the Church in this country is so often lifeless is not that Christians never taste the power and strength of God, it is that, astonishingly, they *lose* the taste for it. So most of this practical section is taken up with ways of holding fast to God's purpose, ways to stay on God's path. Persistence, commitment, attention to detail – none of these things might sound very exciting, but they are among the keys to manisfesting the real excitement of God's miracle-working.

The preparation

First, though, a few basics, starting with this thought: We can all do more with our lives than we are doing at the moment. Rephrasing that slightly, we are all *called* to do more than we are at present doing. And that idea of calling – of God not only *wanting* us to do more but *actually asking* us – brings me to the thing we need before anything else at all: submission. Submission is another of those unpopular concepts these days, not least in church circles. But it is God's way. There is no point in God calling us to do something if we do not listen to Him. And there is no point in listening if we do not do as He asks. That is what submission means, Bonhoeffer said: 'When Christ calls a man He bids him to come and die.' Watchman Nee called it 'handing oneself over to God'. Garibaldi, the great 19th-century Italian leader, stood before thousands of his fellow countrymen and called to them: 'I offer you no wages, no home, no food. . .I only offer you thirst, hunger, forced marches, battle, bloodshed, perhaps even death. But let him who loves his country with all his heart – follow me!' They followed in their tens of thousands. He called for them to sacrifice their present comforts and their desires, that they might grasp a greater glory!

That leads on to a basic checklist, things to watch as you set out in answer to God's calling:

1. Desire to be used.
2. Submit to God and live by His will.
3. Take God as your partner and guide in life.
4. Pray without ceasing.
5. Believe – always have faith.
6. Expect things to work together for good.
7. Forget 'self'.
8. Work hard.
9. Keep a good, kind heart towards people; never get hard or professional.
10. Finally, remember that with the help of Jesus you can achieve what He wants you to – nothing is impossible through Him.

The call

Now I want to look more closely at this sense of call. If one is going to be blessed in working miracles, healing the sick, building churches, the ministry or as a 'normal' Christian, 'one must have a feeling or conviction of God's call', as Watchman Nee put it. Journalists and radio and television interviewers worldwide ask me constantly:

'Why are you in this work?' to which my reply is always:

'Because God called me to it.' I would not have dared to lift a Bible to preach, or lay a hand on a sick person, or even enter a church, unless God Himself had spoken to me.

First, God's call is a personal call

He touched my heart in the second row of the cinema that night in Bristol. As Colossians puts it, He 'delivered us out of the domain of darkness into the kingdom of His dear son'. We are a special breed, the children of God. Dante expresses this in his *Divine Comedy*:

> Think of your breed; for brutish ignorance.
> Your mettle was not made; you were made men,
> To follow after knowledge and excellence. . .

On a friend's desk is a motto. Sometimes I do not look at it, I confess, but I know that it is there. Never a week goes by without this motto – a quotation from Jean Ingelow – challenging me or cheering me. It prompts me to stop trying to do everything and keeps me to my own job:

> I am glad to think I am not bound to make
> the world go right, but only to discover and

to do with cheerful heart the work that God
appoints.

In any walk of life, there are enough obstacles to be
overcome, victories to be won, without us looking
around at work we are not suited for.

Years ago, a violet grew near the trunk of a tree. The
violet was modest. The tree was proud.

'You poor little, helpless, useless thing', said the tree
contemptuously. 'You'll bloom and fade within a few
days. But look at me. I'll stand here for centuries.
You are weak; I am strong. You're worth nothing;
I'm of great value. Don't you feel miserable about
it?'

'Frankly, no', said the violet. 'I can't be a tree, however
much I want to be. So I'm content to be a violet. . .and
folk say I'm rather sweet.'

That very day, a flash of lightning shattered the proud
tree.

After the storm, in the quietness of dusk, a woman
walked that way. She was a mother who had lost her
child. She saw the violet and plucked it; carried it
home and pressed it between the pages of her Bible.
And there it is still, bringing comfort to a white-haired
woman.

If you cannot be a big tree, you can be a little flower
for God. He will still use you as He wills. Step back,
and ask yourself, 'Am I doing God's will?' Look at
your life again. Are you following His purpose for
you?

Recently, I was in a small town and came upon
an artist at work. There he was, in a corner of a
sleepy square, his picture on an easel, his brushes
and paintbox in hand. And it was a good picture,
too.

What intrigued me was the way he stepped back from
the painting every few minutes and looked at it with his

head on one side. I suppose the only way he could really see his work properly was by getting a bit away from it.

I could not help thinking, friend, that you and I need to do something rather like that from time to time. After all, we want to be artists in living, don't we?

Secondly, a call needs patience

Take a pinch of patience, folks,
Mix with work and fun,
Stir a while and add a push,
That's the way it's done.

Pepper up the lot with pluck,
Serve as best you may,
There's my God-Call and recipe
For a happy life.

'The most unhappy man is he that is not patient in adversity, for men are not killed with the adversities they have but with the *impatience* they suffer'. This was written centuries ago on the wall of a cell in the Tower of London. The writing is still clear and the truth shines as brightly now as ever.

You, of course, have your troubles, and it may be that they worry you a great deal. But, it isn't often that the trouble itself is too great. As a rule you can overcome it or, as a last resort, endure it. But it's your impatience and anxiety and rebellion that get you down and wear your spirit.

If only you can be a little more patient. If only you learn somehow to remain calm. . .then it's amazing how little even a big trouble can hurt.

To work out your calling against all odds will be very difficult and need great patience. The old lines are true:

The calling may seem impossible –

A task too big for you;
You 'know' it's much too hard – a job
You simply cannot do!

But here's the wonder and surprise, by God's Grace
Amazing and yet true.
You can do what's impossible,
And do it *finely, too*!

Thirdly you need some push or 'GO'
Once upon a time – so runs a legend – there was a man who, for some reason he couldn't understand, was suddenly arrested, marched off to prison, and flung into a cell.

He sat there with his head in his hands, wondering why such undeserved treatment had been meted out to him, of all men; wondering how many days or months or years he was to be a captive; wondering if the authorities would let him starve, or if they would torture him. . .and all the time he felt terribly, terribly sorry for himself.

At last, for want of something better to do, he tried to loosen the bars at the tiny window. Then he thought of scratching the mortar between the stones. Finally, he gave the door a push. . .and as it swung open easily he walked out and went home.

It seems that there's nothing quite like push.

Fourthly BE POSITIVE
A friend received a letter from a nephew. It seems that the boy was very keen on cricket, and that he'd written to his uncle saying: 'The last time I played for school I'd have made a century if I'd got another 98 runs.' I rather liked that.

It's a matter of which angle you look at life from: Your health is indifferent, or you're pretty well except for an ache or two; you've all the burdens imaginable, or life's a big adventure, really, and if it's hard going so much the better. . . .

In other words, what happens doesn't really matter much. What *does* matter is whether you whine – or crack a joke.

It takes a positive look to see the best.

What I want to go on to deal with now is most vital. So many start out, have a real call, get rich blessings from God, climb mountains, win converts, even get people marvellously healed, see tremendous answer to prayers, see the miraculous, living God working in their lives. . .then suddenly you hear no more of them. They fall by the wayside, are sidetracked, stumble and fall, become disheartened, get weary in well-doing; they give up and lose the precious anointing God gifted them with. I have noted fourteen essential KEYS TO MAINTAINING THE BLESSING IN YOUR WALK WITH GOD. Fourteen qualifications to manifesting God's Grace, power, a ministry with increasing achievements and results, and each one of these has become lacking in many lives. CHERISH THESE, WATCH THESE, MAINTAIN THESE:

1. USE THE GIFT
2. CLING TO GOD's PROMISES
3. GO FOR GOD's HIGHEST FOR YOURSELF
4. KEEP YOUR TRUST STRONG
5. KEEP THANKFUL
6. WATCH SMALL THINGS
7. KEEP CLOSE TO MAN'S NEEDS
8. DO NOT MISJUDGE
9. NEVER TIRE OF PRAYER
10. KEEP THE WORD

1. USE REGULARLY THE GIFT THAT GOD HAS GIVEN YOU

Once upon a time a beggar called at a lonely cottage. The woman said she had no food so the beggar offered to make her some 'nail soup'.

From his pocket he took a nail and put it in a pan of water. Then at intervals, he said, 'You wouldn't have a potato, would you?' 'Or a few bacon rinds?' 'A handful of lentils?' 'A bit of turnip, or a cabbage leaf?'

Yes, the old woman had all these, and one by one they were put in the pot. Soon a delicious broth was done to a turn; and the beggar removed the nail and put it back in his pocket.

'Now eat up your nail soup', he said.

In other words, if you use what you have, you'll never miss what you haven't.

* * *

Niccolò Paganini was, in many eyes, the most famous violinist. He was born in Genoa, and when he died he left his almost magical violin to his native city.

That was as it should be. But Paganini made one curious stipulation. The violin could be seen – but it was never again to be played. Today Paganini's instrument is on show in a glass case. And because it is never used, the wood is perishing. The violin will one day crumble to dust.

This intrigues me greatly, and I suggest that you and I can remain alive, in the proper sense of the word, only as long as the gift is active and the heart deeply concerned about others. If not, like Paganini's violin, the body may live on – but the gift will die.

* * *

Sir Frederick Treves, surgeon to King Edward VII, was once involved in a railway accident. Happily, he escaped unhurt. The injured were laid out on the side of the track, and Sir Frederick did his best to succour them. As he went from one victim to another he was heard to sigh, 'If only I had my instruments'.

It's no use neglecting *the gift then finding in the hour of need that we have no* instruments – no power *to meet them.*

2. CLING TO GOD'S PROMISES

I try to read eight chapters of scripture daily. Read, soak your mind in God's promises, in them is joy, confidence, hope, power.

I wonder if you know the secret of the snowdrop? Out for a walk with my wife, I noticed the little green shoots pushing up.

'D'you know,' I said, 'I just can't understand how such a fragile little flower can stand up to the snow and frosts of winter.'

Lilian smiled and explained. Every evening, just as dusk begins to fall, the snowdrop's head droops a little lower, and its petals close. She told me that, in doing so, it imprisons within its bell some of the daytime warmth. And the amazing thing is that, even in the hour just before dawn, when the night is at its coldest, the air cradled in the snowdrop's petals can be several degrees warmer than the air surrounding it. This is why the snowdrop can survive the bitterest winter nights and the coldest frosts.

145

It is a parable of life too. For surely it is when life is at its coldest and darkest that we must cling to the warmth of blessings that have been and believe in the promise of sunshine yet to be.

3. GO FOR GOD'S HIGHEST FOR YOURSELF.

Tozer said – 'nothing deforms and twists the soul more than a low or unworthy conception of God'.

A friend of ours spent a few lovely days in the Cairngorms. He climbed a hill or two, and there, while he rested and enjoyed the view, up came a young couple. The girl was in a bad temper, complaining they ought never to have tried to climb that steep slope on such a hot day, and it was all the young man's fault, and she was going down. And down she went, slithering a bit.

Within minutes an elderly man and his wife, both taking their time about the adventure, came slowly uphill, pausing often to admire the view and get their breath, chatting pleasantly and obviously enjoying every minute.

My friend comments – Same steep climb. Same weather. Same difficulties. One party mad. The other glad. One failed. The other reached the top. Isn't this life?

It is as we lift up or visualize and reach our highest conception of God, that we become the purest, holiest and highest for Him. Some give in on the climb – others reach the heights of Him and for Him.

4. KEEP YOUR TRUST STRONG

I like the story of the Mum on her way to meet her son Donald – who had only just started school. Suddenly she realised she was ten minutes late. She hurried to the school gates. Not a soul about. She went indoors anxiously. There in the hall was Donald happily 'helping' the janitor.

'Sorry, dear', murmured a contrite Mum. 'I met somebody. You weren't worried, were you?' Donald beamed.

'No', he said. 'I knew you'd come – you said you would!'

That's what I call faith!

* * *

Once when the Church of Christ was under severe Roman persecution by Nero, the apostle Peter wrote to Christians scattered all over the Roman provinces, to encourage them.

He had seen Christ in the flesh, walked with Him, eaten with Him, watched Him do great miracles, and had even witnessed His transfiguration.

How did he encourage those believers? Did he tell them things were much better in the old days? Did he harp back to the days of Christ's walking on water, and inspire them with such words as: 'You should have seen it'?

No. Peter lifted his pen and wrote those fabulous words: 'Whom having not seen, you love. . . . Though now you see him not, yet believing, you rejoice with joy unspeakable and full of glory: receiving the end of your faith, even the salvation of your souls. . .which things the angels desire to look into (1 Peter 1:8, AV).

Faith in an unseen Christ has a vigour, an independence of all circumstances, a power to defy attempts to extinguish it, a buoyancy, a heavenward ardour, a love, a depth, a height, which faith in a seen Christ could never have had.

'Blessed', said the Saviour, 'are those who have not seen, yet believe.'

That night I came to Christ in the meeting at the cinema in Bristol, I did what Charles Wesley did 250 years ago, I 'laid my reasonings at Jesus's feet. . .' The moment within my heart when I learned to yield to Him I felt what the great English poet felt – 'the wild winds hushed, the angry deep (within) sank like a little child to sleep. . .'

O to learn to rest in Him. This victory of faith is claimed on the strength of what God has said and done in His word. Faith is a philosophy of life, not just when we want something badly. It is a system of living. It is diametrically opposed to the secular thinking of our age. . .

Faith sees the invisible, believes the incredible, and receives the impossible, as the old saying goes. It means believing what God says solely because *He said* it to us. Abraham and Isaac all started on God's naked word, risked all on God's word, submitted to the fact that what He said He would do. What we read we must believe, it is not only true but practicably reliable for our generation. Believing is to stake everything, your very life, on the fact He is true to His words. Dr Martin Lloyd Jones said believing is 'to take the bare word and act upon it'. The urgent, glorious, eternal, transforming Gospel is applicable, every bit of it, for today.

We must believe by acting, practising it. A Chinese student got saved in London and wrote home in broken English and got mixed up – 'I am reading the Word of God and BEHAVING IT' . . .well not far out; we must live it, be an example, act on it. A saying the Wiltshire preachers had when I was a boy was – 'Faith never stands around with its hands in its pockets. . .'

I love the book of Habakkuk, a prophet of trust, faith, revival (see chapter 3: 7–19)

'Yes,' Habakkuk prays, 'I know that judgement is coming on us. But, Lord, I trust You in the midst of the whole thing. I trust You to act. I trust You to work out Your purposes. I will trust You through thick and thin.' Then he comes out with the most joyful affirmation of divine sovereignty one can possibly read anywhere: 'Though the fig tree does not bud and there are no grapes on the vines, though the olive crop fails and the fields produce no food, though there are no sheep in the pen and no cattle in the stalls, yet I will rejoice in the Lord, I will be joyful in God my Saviour. The Sovereign Lord is my strength.'

We can best summarize the attitude of Habakkuk by asking some questions. Do we doubt? Are we troubled by the silence of God? Do we doubt because of disappointments? Do problems confuse us? Somebody has said that, given the world we live in, if God is God He is not good – and if God is good He isn't God. That shows a very shallow understanding of who God is. But that is where many people are. They have doubts. One more question: If you have doubts, will you wait? Will you wait on God and trust in Him? You should, because if you consider the alternatives they are too unspeakably horrible!

As you are waiting on God, are you being faithful? Are you full of faith? Are you trusting Him where you can't see? Will you trust in Him where you don't have all the answers? Will you still have that firm rock under your feet even though there are all kinds of doubts? Faith is the very basis of life. Try living without faith and you will discover you can't.

One day I got in a little plane to make a flight to a preaching appointment, from one island to another in New Zealand. The guy who was to fly the aircraft said it would take us one hour and ten minutes to get there. I believed him, and got into the plane. On the way home we were in the overcast all the way. We couldn't see a thing – we just trusted the instruments. Then a voice spoke to us on the radio, telling us to descend from 7,000 to 2,700 feet. The voice promised us we would come out of the overcast, and we did. The minute we came into the clear at 2,700 feet a runway appeared right in front of us. We trusted the voice, we trusted the instruments, I trusted the pilot, I trusted that plane.

That is how life operates. Do you ever trust God?

* * *

One evening a visitor who had called to see a farmer said goodbye and opened the door to the yard where his car was parked. Standing near the car was the farmer's son, a boy of ten or twelve. He was holding a ball of string.

'What's the idea?' asked the guest.

'Flying my kite', was the reply.

The visitor looked up, but could see no kite – only the stars twinkling in the night sky. 'How do you know your kite is up there?', he inquired.

'Easy', said the boy. 'I can feel it tugging at the string'.

And that is how some of us know there is a God – we feel His presence. *We have the tug of the string of faith, which ties us to Him*!

5. KEEP A THANKFUL SPIRIT

There's more than a smile in this story of a five-year-old who, for the first time in his life, was taught at school to say grace before meals.

One day at tea-time he bowed his head, clasped his hands, and repeated the children's grace: 'Thank You for the food we eat. . .' His father, who had little time for such things, took him to task. 'Look here', he said to his son, 'I'm the one who pays for the food. It's me you should be thanking, not God.'

The boy said nothing. At tea-time next day, when the family had gathered round the table, he bowed his head again. 'Thank you, Daddy, for my food', he began. Then he added, 'And thank you, God, for my Daddy. . .'

6. WATCH SMALL THINGS IN YOUR LIFE

A man I read about told how as a boy he lived in Brazil for a time. That was long ago, but he still remembered with affection the Negro who cooked for them. One day he found the boy kneeling on the sandy garden path. He was stroking a snake only four inches long. The Negro's eyes almost started out of his head, and with a sudden push he bowled him over backwards, shouting, 'Run!'

The boy obeyed, and in the safety of the kitchen the cook explained: 'Big, large snake, him dangerous, but you see him come and you can fast move away. But that leetle fellow, him small and you not afraid. There is trouble. Him bite. Him poison. You die. Very sad!'

Looking back, it all seemed a parable. You recognize the huge serpent for what it is, but the small snake seems harmless till it is too late. . . .

Materials things, ease, ambition, illicit friendships, lack of honesty in small things, can creep up on us and *dethrone God and His power. Small things are vital.*

There is a story of a businessman whose love of money was ruining his life. One day he called on his minister and argued with him about a point he had made in his sermon. The minister, who knew his visitor's failing, opened a Bible, pointed to the word 'God', and asked, 'Can you see that?'

'Of course I can', was the impatient reply.

The minister took a penny and placed it over the word. Then he asked, 'Can you see it now?'

The businessman was silenced!

7. NEVER LOSE SIGHT OF SOCIETY'S NEED

You will always have power if you keep close to people's need. God will match the challenge with the grace to meet the need! '*If I have a great need of Christ, I have a great Christ to meet my need*', so the old saying goes.

She lived in a very pleasant part of the town and she didn't seem to have any worries. Then came that lovely spring evening: the garden a picture; birds singing everywhere; folk enjoying a foretaste of summer. As she walked along the avenue she stopped to chat with a neighbour; she admired somebody's tulips; she waved her hand to a girl who was riding off to tennis. . .and she drowned herself in the river ten minutes later.

That woman walked in the sunshine to her death. Suppose somebody she met had been quick enough to detect the hidden despair and persuaded her to come in and have a cup of tea. Such a little thing might have accomplished so much.

But *they did not* see her despair and heartache. The world is crying for the love of God; screaming in the dark *for* help from *the Lord! Recognize it! Keep close to it!* and you will manifest great power and grace *to meet it*.

I arrived in the French city of Nancy to conduct a mission, a great metropolis of some 250,000 people, with only three small evangelical churches. The Assemblies of God was the largest with about eighty people. The pastor had faith in taking a five hundred-seater hall, with only about thirty to forty workers to help. The first night about one hundred and fifty came, among them many sick people. One little group were Turkish Muslims, and they had never been in a Christian meeting in their lives. They were immigrants who worked in the town. The local government officials gave them an interpreter to sit with them to tell them what I was saying in their own language. Also, I had my French interpreter on the platform with me, thus two translators for two different groups. God anointed the message as I preached of the 'one Saviour for all mankind' Our Lord Jesus Christ. . .the non-Christian interpreter with eyebrows raised, just told them everything I said! Many signified they would like to know Jesus at the close of the meeting when we had a time of counselling and leading people to our Lord.

Then came time for laying on of hands for the sick. Among the folk who came forward were a number of the Turkish friends, including a little boy of about eight years of age, deaf and dumb, who had never spoken in his life! I touched him, I asked Jesus to reveal Himself as the living God of love to these dear lost dark people. As I prayed, the little boy looked up and turned his head all around, holding his ears, the noise of people praying just overcame him as his ears were opened. Then we started him with the alphabet, then through the interpreter we asked him to respond to the language of his parents, soon they were speaking to him and he began to utter letters, words in Turkish, it was clearly *a startling miracle*, incredible to everyone. To these people it was unexplainable, they looked to Jesus straight away. . .they asked for more prayers and help, and at the next meeting hundreds of them came and the great hall was crammed night after night.

At the Turkish follow-up meeting when we had tea and a fellowship to encourage them and all the new converts, four hundred or more came to hear more of going on with God. Signs and wonders were a great breakthrough amongst these people. *Why such a move, not known in Europe amongst Turkish people before, with one of the most closed races on earth? I believe it was because the gift was placed in the midst of the need. . . A secret of spiritual power and exercising the miraculous. . .is in keeping in a place where there is plenty of need surrounding you and facing you! Your gift is not for yourself, whatever it is, it is for the world and the Church*. Keep where the sinners are, keep where the sick and incurable are, keep where there are plenty of lost souls, pagan people, keep close to people's need, and the *gift will grow by its using...*

Recently at the Keswick convention I heard of a Christian who was buying an ice cream just outside the tent, perhaps 10,000 people crowding the streets, and he asks the ice cream man – 'Are you saved?' The man said, 'I don't think I am. It's nice of you to enquire after me. I have been coming here for twenty years to this convention, sold ice creams to tens of thousands, but no one has ever asked me that question'! How sad, we must not think only of our needs, but keep an eye out for the need of others...!!

A preacher was ministering at a country church. He stayed that night at a remote farm. Just before supper, the farmer said: 'I must go out to deliver a lamb, would you like to come?' The preacher, fascinated, agreed, and they went with a torch out through the back of the farm, in the cold of the night, into a large barn where there were many sheep. In one corner a mother sheep was about to give birth. The farmer knelt down, stroked the sheep's head and in a few minutes, in the midst of blood and waste in the smelly straw, had delivered the baby safely and set the mother down to rest. As he did so, the mother licked the farmer's hand.

Later, after he had returned to the comfort of the farmhouse and had got washed up and warm and had a good big supper, the preacher asked the farmer: 'Why did the mother sheep kiss your hand?' The wise old farmer looked up and smiled, and in a deep Devonian voice *'Because I was there in the sheep's time of need...'*

Many today are desperate in their needs, they are waiting for a helping, loving hand, for a Christ-glorifying message, for God's words of comfort, strength, upliftment, peace and release from us. *Begin to manifest god's power to help, bless, heal, deliver, change people.*

8. DO NOT MISJUDGE OTHERS

Give others the benefit of the doubt. Look for the best in them. Scripture says – 'in honour preferring one another': 'do unto others as ye would have them do unto you': 'esteem others greater than yourself'.

Don't jump to conclusions!

When George and his wife were on holiday they often took their grandchildren to play in the park. They noticed an old lady who always seemed to be there – poorly dressed, and over her arm a battered old basket, covered with a tattered cloth. As she moved about, she stooped down from time to time, picked up something, and put it in the basket under the cloth.

One day, one of the children mislaid one of his little treasures. Though Grandpa and Granny searched too, it couldn't be found. They wondered about the old woman. So George approached her and asked if he might see in the basket. She did not reply, but drew aside the cloth. There, to his surprise, he saw rusty tins, broken glass and sharp stones. George was embarrassed and offered his apologies. But the old woman just smiled. 'I never had any children of my own,' she said wistfully, 'but I like to do my bit to keep the little ones safe.'

I repeat – Don't be too quick to judge!

The thought is prompted by an incident I heard about in Bournemouth. Some time ago a lady entered a restaurant and took a seat at a table where two punk rockers with brightly coloured hair were polishing off the last of a big dinner. A moment later an old couple came to the table, took the other two seats and ordered a cup of tea and a bun. The two youths finished their dinner and left. After a few minutes the waitress set two big plates of meat, veg and potatoes before the old couple.

'No, no, miss,' they said, 'you've made a mistake'. The girl smiled.

'When those two lads left', she said 'they told me to see you had a proper dinner and they paid for it in advance.' The old couple looked at each other, too overcome to speak. Then quietly they explained it was their golden wedding day. They had come to Bournemouth for the day, but couldn't afford a cooked meal. The punks looked a sight but their thoughtfulness gave an old couple their most precious memory of a golden day.

There is a lot of criticism, judgement, jealous spirits among people – even among Christian workers in the Church today and *amongst ministers*. Do not misjudge!

9. NEVER TIRE OF REAL PRAYER

No single truth is more important than this one. We must learn genuine prayer.

It has often been told how Sir Walter Scott wrote many of his books to pay off a debt incurred by the publishing house of which he was a partner.

The task was monumental, undermining his strength in the end, even if bringing him fame. He related how, in all his anxiety, he found strength and calm with new resolution, when, after dinner, he would stroll down the garden to the home of his coachman and listen to the humble Scot raise his voice in leading his family in nightly worship. Robbie Burns too, confessed that the words he loved best in all the language were, 'Let us Worship God'. And that 'The Cotter's Saturday Night' was inspired for him by the habit of his father in conducting family worship.

In all the restlessness of our times, strength for the day may be found in that brief hour of prayer.

Prayer is so misunderstood.

The little boy who was sitting in the visitors' gallery of the Senate building in Washington, saw the Chaplain arrive to open the session in prayer, and asked his Dad – 'Is that man going to pray for the Senate, Daddy?' His father looked up and replied – 'Not exactly son, what he does is look around at the Senate, then he prays for the *country*. . .'!

Some people do not seem to think God can manage all our problems. For instance, take the little boy, praying on the back seat of his Mum's car which had broken down. Unable to get it going, she heard her tiny son praying – 'Dear God, help Mum to get the car going. If you can't come then send my Dad to do the job. . .'

I LOVE THE POET'S WORDS -

There is a place where Thou canst touch the eyes
Of blinded men to instant perfect sight:
There is a place where Thou canst say, 'Arise!'
To dying captives, bound in chains of night.
There is a place where Thou canst reach the store
Of hoarded gold and free it for the Lord:
There is a place upon some distant shore
Where thou canst send the worker and the Word:
There is a place where heaven's resistant power
Responsive moves to thine insistent plea:
There is a place – a silent trusting hour –
Where God Himself descends and fights for thee.
Where is that secret place?
Dost thou ask where?
O soul, it is the secret place of prayer!

FOR REAL PRAYER -

Real prayer makes the shallow soul – big
   prayer makes the foolish   – wise
   it makes the ignorant   – intelligent
   it makes the slothful   – busy
   prayer makes the weak   – strong

it makes the indifferent	– zealous
it makes the unbeliever	– trustful
and the craven	– courageous

I thank God I learnt to pray early in my Christian life, as those earlier days were spent in the Salvation Army. One of my peers was old Alfred Cox, a life-long Salvationist, an old timer, from whom, from the moment as a young convert I came under his wing, I learned at the 7.30 a.m. prayer meetings how to begin to intercede. It was called in those days 'knee drill'! If I missed for some reason, I would have old 'Coxy' after me! He would soon have his hand on my shoulder saying that my place was in the prayer meetings. Old Alfred was severe, sour at times, but strict in his prayer times. I learned something in that early discipline.

Prayer is a discipline, but it is more than that – it is a joyous discovery. I am able to meet the day with confidence when I have spent time with God. Individually and corporately we need to rediscover the value and power of prayer; for both individual and corporate life, like a watch, has a tendency to run down.

Pray at all times in the Spirit, with all prayer and supplication.

The practice and art of prayer must be foremost on our list of spiritual priorities. Reservoirs of power are at our disposal – but only as we pray. Many Christians, however, expect results without any practice of the art. Would we not think a person foolish who played a musical instrument only occasionally, expecting to tune in to music and become the instrument of music without taking time to practise?

The main direction of faith is to enable us to exercise a successful prayer life, it is more important to pray than even to worship. Secondly it is to bring us under the lordship of Christ in our communion with Him. And thirdly, to keep us in the Holy Place of continuous yielding, brokenness unto the Living God.

A little boy who heard someone play 'God save the Queen' on a mouth organ at a fairground bought one, and when he got home and failed to get a tune out of it, burst into tears and told his mother: 'The man cheated me, there is no "God save the Queen" in this mouth organ.' Many of us just as foolishly believe we can get ready-made spiritual results without the practice of prayer. If we spent half as much time in learning the art of prayer as we do in learning any other art, we would get ten times the results.

Some people use God like little Mary just before her holidays. . . Wee Mary is only four, and every night at bedtime she kneels to pray under the watchful eye of her mother. The other night, on the eve of the family holiday, Mary said her prayers as usual, but after completing them she remained on her knees.

There was a momentary silence, and then she said – 'Goodbye, God. You won't be hearing from me for the next four weeks. I'm going on my holidays.' No wonder little Mary's mother smiled as she tucked her daughter into bed.

A padre in the RAF was walking across the tarmac with a pilot of a fighter plane who asked him if he ever prayed – 'Oh yes, padre, I pray when I'm flying'. The padre went on – 'But I never see you in my chapel services', the pilot replied – 'Oh no, when I'm on the ground I can manage myself. . . !'

Listen!

On the way home from church one Sunday a young man remarked to the minister, 'It's all right you talking about the voice of God and the voice of conscience. Well, I must admit I've never once heard any such voice.'

'I believe you', was the reply. 'But I sometimes wonder if the reason why many folk don't hear the voice of God is because they're making too much noise themselves.'

Maybe, folks, if you and I were quiet now and then, really quiet for a few minutes. . .we might hear the voice of God telling us what to do and assuring us of strength to do it.

A young woman on the verge of a breakdown was told by her doctor: 'Jane, I don't know what to do for you. You had better go home and get on your knees and pray.' Surprising advice for a general practitioner to give! When the girl returned home, she told her mother what the doctor had said, and asked: 'Mother, don't you think that was a strange thing for him to say?' Her mother said: 'Yes, it was, but why don't you try it?' She did – and within an hour was a new person. The doctor was obviously in the Spirit in this girl's case – it was the right diagnosis and the right prescription.

Let us listen!
'Whether it is good or evil, we will obey the voice of the Lord our God. . .that it may be well with us. . .' (Jeremiah 42:1–22)

The growing Christian is one who listens, who learns and who obeys. If he does not approach God to listen The Voice will grow silent, and spiritual paralysis will set in. A minister stood up in a small prayer meeting some years ago and said: 'God has shown me tonight that I must shift the emphasis in my life from talking to taking.' He had caught on to one of the greatest lessons of the Christian life – receptivity.

'. . . Then Samuel said, "Speak, for your servant is listening".' 1 Samuel 3:1–19.

All commerce with heaven begins in prayer, but like all communication it is a two-way process – we talk to God and He talks to us. Prayer is meant to be a dialogue, not a monologue.

I am amazed at how many Christians I meet who, when I ask them about their prayer life, tell me that although they spend a lot of time talking to God, they rarely pause to let God talk to them. One of the best pieces of advice I ever received was from a man who said: 'After you have talked to God in prayer, relax and say to Him, "Father, have You anything to say to me?" Then I listen.' Prime the pump of your spirit and get in the mood for prayer; give God an opportunity to illuminate some word or passage to your heart and thus make you aware of His personal interest in your affairs. Christians who defect do so primarily because they have failed to establish and maintain clear lines of communication with God. They do not listen. A church poster I saw the other day put it: 'If at this moment God seems far away – guess who moved!'

Prayer and the neglect of it is one of the prime reasons behind spiritual defection. The less we pray, the less motivated we will be to live and behave as a Christian should. 'I've let down on my prayer time,' said a missionary to me the other day, 'and I'm suffering defeat after defeat in my Christian life.' Is it any wonder?

'But you dear friends build yourselves up in your most holy faith and pray in the Holy Spirit.'

God speaks through prayer to us!

O Father, as I kneel in Your presence today, help me to realize that prayer is not just me speaking to You, but You speaking to me. Speak to me today – in the same clear way that You spoke to Your Son. For His dear Name's sake I ask it. Amen

Ethel Roming Fuller says concerning this matter of whether God can speak to us in prayer:

If radio's slim fingers can pluck a melody
From night – and toss it over a continent or sea;
If the petalled white notes of a violin
Are blown across the mountains or the city din;
If songs like crimsoned roses, are culled from thin blue
　　air,
Why should mortals wonder if God speaks in prayer?

Open up the lines of communication with God once more and talk to Him in prayer. Pour out before Him all your feelings – the discouragement, the doubts, the despair. Hold nothing back. The more real and honest you are, the more God can do for you. Martin Luther once said: 'The first rule of prayer is to be honest.' It is. Experience has shown that something happens when a person is honest with God.

His power comes through prayer to us.

The motto outside a church in Missouri USA reads – *'We believe that the power behind us, is greater than the task before us'!*

We must not be satisfied with half-hearted prayers. David Shepherd, the famous TV wild-life artist, was painting on the screen in a demostration, he finished his fine picture then stepped back and said: 'I'm not satisfied, no not really satisfied, when you are. . .*you make no prayers. . .*'

Someone said to me – 'When the conditions are right God does not say yes to our prayers, He is not really saying no, He never says 'no', He merely does not say 'yes' when the idea is not the best for us!

He does not say 'yes' when the idea is absolutely wrong for us!
He does not say 'yes' when it may help you, but create problems for others.

The Bible makes it clear that God does not answer all selfish, begging, childish, crying and pitiful pleadings. Some have totally selfish, materialistic requests, doubtful and cynical prayers. Prayer is not a scream or a scheme to get things. It is relationship with God, which fosters growth of spirituality, a spiritual exercise whereby we draw ourselves to God, where we can get into closer harmony with God's great plan and purpose and peace for us. Prayer is not always to give you what you want, but turn you into the person God wants you to be!

Prayer gives us surviving power. . .

We need to meditate, turn over in our minds, think of the Scriptures, the thoughts of God. We have a media bombardment today. Christian faith, marriage, stability, morals, truth, fear of the Lord, justice are all under attack and under great pressure. Learn to get peace from prayer!

A prayerful man asked – 'Do you count sheep to go to sleep?' He replied 'No! . . .I talk to the shepherd. . .' Talk, speak with, share with Jesus in prayer; you'll even sleep better. When I lay my head down to sleep, far away from loved ones, in the heart of South–East Asia, bitten by fifteen mosquitoes a night in Malaysia, lizards running over my bed, with mice under the bed in Belgium, the cry of the Mullahs at 5.00 in the morning in the Middle East calling the Muslims to prayer, at seven hundred miles-an-hour in Jumbos, in trains from the North of Scotland all night, shunting and creaking, in the backs of cars driven over mountain roads in the South of France. . .when I pray, I seem to be able to sleep anywhere on my travels for Jesus!

A badge on a teenager I saw at the end of one of my great rallies in Melbourne, Australia, recently read – 'beware! I'm dangerous. . .I've been waiting on God. . .'

Let us wait and hear from him.

Those who find the idea of listening for God's voice in prayer too challenging should remember that this is not the only way God speaks. He also speaks to us by quickening our hearts to some word or passage of Scripture. That is why it is important to have a Bible close at hand when you pray. Ideally, it is best to begin your prayer time with the Bible and also end with it. Beginning with the Bible helps.

Pray today: 'Forgive me, dear Lord, that my prayer life is built around the attitude, "Listen, Lord, Your servant

163

is speaking" rather than, "Speak, Lord, Your servant is listening." Help me to get my attitude right – today. In Jesus's Name. Amen.'

Pray today: 'O Lord teach me to receive, so I come again and say, "Teach me to pray." I want to emerge from my prayer times more alive to life, more alive to others – and above all, more alive to you.'

Prayer is life-changing and life-creating. All the great Christian leaders of the past have been men and women of prayer. Martin Luther said: 'I have so much business I cannot get on without spending three hours daily in prayer.' John Wesley once declared, 'God does nothing but in answer to prayer' – and backed up his belief by devoting two hours a day to the sacred exercise.

The great Methodist preacher, Dr W.E. Sangster, once wrote: 'Part of the secret of progress in the spiritual life is to harness the mind in prayer in the quest for Christ.'

'Where your treasure is there your heart will be also' (Matthew 6:21; NIV). Your treasure must be in Christ – wholly and supremely – let it be speaking to him and receiving *from him* in prayer.

Often circumstances of life get people into an attitude of readiness for praying. Look at Habakkuk's response in the Old Testament. In his third chapter, he begins by requesting divine mercy: 'Lord,' he says, 'I have heard of your fame, I stand in awe of your deeds, O Lord. Renew them in our day, in our time make them known, in wrath remember mercy' (3:2). Then Habakkuk proceeds to pray for his beleaguered people. The Babylonians are bearing down on them, tragedy is inevitable. Confronted with the whole situation, the prophet prays and pleads for divine mercy. Then he carefully recounts divine history. He remembers what God has done and *stands* on His goodness!

Moses prayed for the people. . . 'don't let them be lost. *Blot me out of your book. . .but save them*.' What passion, what praying! Moses gave them a change, stood in the gap, was willing to suffer so that their needs might be met: 'save them, give them a chance, blot me out instead of them,' he cried. We need to plead with God, weep rivers of tears from the depths of our souls like this. . .

Some people think prayer is like the amazing new tractor seen at an agricultural show recently. By just pressing a button, the tractor went up and down the field, pulling the plough, ploughed the whole field, released the plough, left the field, went up the country road, turned into the farm and put itself away in the barn, without the farmer even getting out of bed! *All at the press of a button*! Some people think prayer is like that: a press-button God, He will do it all, with no cost, no sacrifice by us at all! *Prayer is not easy*.

God wants to answer. He said to Abraham – 'Shall I hide from Abraham what I want to do'? (Genesis 18:17). God wants to inspire us in prayer. There is such a satisfaction in prayer, such a joy in waiting in and for God. 'If my people shall humble themselves, pray, seek my face. . .then will I hear from heaven. . .and heal their land. . . (2 Chronicles 7:14).

When Dr Cho recently arrived at the First Baptist Church, Dallas, Texas, to preach on the Sunday morning, he arrived at 7.15 for the 8.0 a.m. service. He was invited, with his assistant brother, Cha, to join the prayer meeting and he heartily agreed. Brother Cha pointing out that Dr Cho had already spent three hours in prayer before the service began – what power was on that man of God as he preached to the vast crowd that morning!

10. KEEP THE WORD

Two centuries ago, Dr Johnson was talking to James Boswell regarding Christianity: 'Sir, ours is a book religion.' Four thousand times in the Old Testament the phrase is used 'thus saith the Lord, God *has spoken*.'

Kierkegaard, the Danish philosopher, said – 'The Bible settles what Christianity is.'

I was reading the other day about that fine Scotsman, John Rennie, the civil engineer, who died as long ago as 1821. John was born poor. But how quickly he made a stir in the world! He was for a short time linked up with James Watt. Then he began building canals. He became famous for his docks and harbours, especially his stupendous Plymouth breakwater, a mile long.

He built bridges at Kelso and Musselburgh, Waterloo Bridge, London and Southwark Bridge. There seemed to be no limit to his originality and resource. But what I liked best about the account I read of this famous engineer was this phrase: 'The distinguishing characteristics of Rennie's work were firmness and solidity, and what he has done has stood the test of time.'

God's word stands the test of time

Dr E.V. Rieu, an agnostic, translated the Scriptures into modern English. He found it, he said, 'extraordinarily alive'; 'it changed me'! The poet Coleridge said: 'I believe the Bible is God's word, because *it finds me. . .*' You see, the Scripture makes God real to us. Erasmus in the fifteenth century said: 'It makes Christ so real, as if he stood before my eyes.'

I try to read up to eight chapters of Scripture every day. Soak yourself in it. The greatest intercessors and prayer warriors have been those who have been filled with the Word of God. John Bunyan said, that as long as he had his Bible, it was all he wanted, in those lonely years of exile, for twelve winters locked up. But, as he declared, the 'Word of God was not bound'! Luther said – in his titanic struggle with the powers of Europe, who would have crushed the 'baby of the Reformation at its birth', in Scripture are the little daily breathers. . . It was spiritual fresh air to the great man.

GOD'S WORD IS VITAL TO MINISTERING THE
    MIRACULOUS
GOD'S WORD GIVES US VICTORY
GOD'S WORD GIVES US LIFE!

A story is told of Sir Christopher Wren that while
building a London church he planned a roof which
was somewhat daring. Several envious architects 'talked
down' this particular bit of Sir Christopher's work, and
certain church authorities, intimidated by the critics,
compelled the architect to make the church roof safe by
adding two pillars.

Sir Christopher reasoned, explained and pleaded, but
the authorities would have things their way. So the two
pillars were duly erected.

It was not until fifty years later that a surprising
discovery was made. The two pillars were several inches
too short – and therefore did just nothing to help to
support the roof. It was as if Sir Christopher had said:
'What I have built I have built. It will stand.'

God's word stands unfailing for us at this hour.
Memorize it, in it we have certainty, assurance, power,
purity, faith, inner strength and confidence. *It is dynamite, it is not merely a good, great book, it is not harmless
and respectable, it is powerful, dangerous, dynamic, the
man of the book is indestructible, invincible*.

11. BEAT DISCOURAGEMENT

This is no doubt the main reason why most men and
women give up and go back. Such things as other
Christians who will not grasp the vision; a secularized
society that is so indifferent; impatience with God's
timing; and extreme trials. . .all these discourage. Also,
despair as a leader, through the circumstances of life,
or despondence as a parent or with your family life,
disappointment with fellow ministers, elders or your

church leaders: all these can sap, tire one, and cause breakdown, failure, resignation, doubt and surrender.

Rudyard Kipling summed up encouraging one another as – 'helping some lame dog over a stile'! A nervous little boy whose family were forced out of their home when he was seven had to work to support them. At nine his mother died, at twenty-two he lost his job as a shop clerk. At twenty-three he became a partner in a small shop, but soon his business partner died leaving him a huge debt which took him years to repay. At twenty-eight he asked the girl he loved to marry him and she said 'No'. Two years later he had a nervous breakdown. At forty-one his 4-year-old son died; at forty-nine he lost his second run for the Senate of the USA. He was despised by multitudes, misunderstood, had periods of deep depression, was snubbed, ignored, laughed at. At fifty-six he was gunned down and died in a tiny anteroom. Yet one of the most famous memorials in the world is built to him in Washington DC, the huge Lincoln monument – his name, of course, ABRAHAM LINCOLN.

At fifty-one his life had been an utter waste and failure, and he was on the scrap heap, yet this man in the last three years of his life became the greatest US president who ever lived.

How did he beat discouragement?
One night a friend of his was staying with him in the White House and happened to catch a glimpse of him through an open door kneeling before an open Bible. He heard him say: 'O thou great God, who heard Solomon in the night when he prayed and cried for wisdom, *hear me.*' He went on: 'I cannot guide these people, I cannot guide the affairs of this country without Thy help. O Lord, hear me and save this nation'. He learned to wait for God, and the Union was preserved. His trials turned him into a great man.

Discouragements hit us from different directions. As a potential leader, evangelist, church worker, or member, house group leader, deacon, openair worker, church helper or minister, you see no way forward in your present position. I know of an old preacher, twenty-five years in a church which only had a handful of people. You would never put him on the platform of a church growth conference! Retired, he went over to France to see a relative who settled there, got invited to speak at a little local church, and miracles happened! He has moved around France ever since, for the past four years in great power, winning souls, teaching, rebuilding churches. . .moving in power in his 70s! Wigglesworth was in his late 50s–60s before he moved in power; I know a pastor in his 40s who had church after church, every one a failure. He went down and down, and finally finished in Kent without a church. He went across the Channel, and suddenly his ministry took off on the continent. In very hard countries, one after another has seen outstanding miracles of healing, churches rebuilt, and many won to Christ in the past year or two.

It is so easy to be discouraged. It is one of Satan's greatest weapons to hinder our spiritual development, and it robs us of assurance of faith. Nevertheless, you are not alone if, as you read this, you feel discouraged. At the age of thirty, Florence Nightingale said, 'My God, what will become of me? I have no desire but to die.' But, when she died sixty years later, she had made a mark on medical history.

We do well to bear in mind that ministry for God is going to cost us. Our Lord knew a cost in His healing ministry – 'power had gone out from him' (Mark 5:30). No wonder there were those times when He has tired or fell asleep after His exertions. Elijah, a real 'lion of a man', was unable to cope with the threat of one woman because he was tired. He was afraid (I Kings 19:).

169

Maybe you identify with his sense of hopelessness. Yet, in the mercy of God there are no impossible situations – only people who have lost hope in them.

A word at the right moment helps
The cook in a noble house gave her notice, even though she was well-paid. When she was asked why, she replied:

'When the meal is good the Duke and Duchess never praise me; when it is bad they never blame me. It is just not worthwhile. Encouragement and rebuke would be so helpful.' *A word in season would have saved her!*

A pastor made a comment about my ministry, about seven years ago, and it got back to me. 'He's had his day, he's nearly finished, no one will want him in another six months, Melvin Banks' ministry will have flipped out shortly.' But the truth is, in the past seven years it has grown more rapidly, reached more masses of the unsaved; I have seen far more miracles, travelled to more nations (twenty in that time) have been invited to go and preach the Gospel and reached more millions with the message of Jesus than in the previous twenty-eight years! *Do not listen to the wet blankets – have enough fire to dry them out!*

God gave Moses a clear instruction concerning the training of Joshua. He said, 'Encourage him, because he will lead Israel'.

Different folk get discouraged by various facets. Some are beaten by the circumstances of life. In his last journals David Livingstone wrote: 'We punted six hours to a little islet, a pitiless pelting rain came on, the wind tore the text out of our hands, the loads are all soaked – nothing earthly will make me give up my work in despair, I encourage myself in the Lord my God.'

* * *

Leaders are always in the thick of conflict, sometimes the objects of it and at other times the cause of it. Leadership is a privilege, but carries with it tremendous pressures and responsibilities. Do you feel discouraged with the people you minister to? You may see Christians with great potential throwing it all away. Perhaps you feel, or have been, let down by people you trusted. It is not impossible that you are wounded by the thoughtless words of members of your own Church.

We must persist and fight life's disasters –

> Something hits you very hard,
> Lays you quite flat out
> Makes you sure life isn't much
> To write home about;
> Hit so badly, any guy
> Feels like lying down to die.
>
> You can lie down NOW, of course,
> Lie there flat as flat;
> But there's something you can do
> Well worth two of that;
> Up, and fight and keep right on
> Till the things that hit have gone!

A preacher friend of mine was once staying in a house he had never been into before, a beautiful farmhouse. During the night he wanted a drink of water so he got out of bed and tried to find the way to the door in the pitch dark. He found a handle and turned it, opened the door and stepping right into a wardrobe, he really felt stupid, shut up inside a cupboard, unable to get out. Shut up. Smothered with someone's suits and dresses, with a lady's hat fallen on his head at 2.00 o'clock in the morning! When we have got down, trapped in despair, we have to learn to laugh and get out of our 'corners' or 'cupboards' of despair, learn to smile again, get up and get going. . .

God is committed to encouraging us and demonstrates that in Jesus Christ. Let us take our encouragement from that and be challenged to encourage others because of it.

171

Then some are discouraged by their children letting them down.

A mother invited a large number of visitors to Sunday lunch. She asked her youngest son to say grace. He replied, 'I don't know what to say Mummy.' 'Yes you do, just say what you have heard Mummy say.' He looked surprised and then said, 'O Lord, why did I ever invite this lot to lunch?' You have tried to bring your family up in the fear and honour of God. . .

They may have drifted from the faith. Perhaps a daughter or grandchild has gone wrong morally. A son is into drugs, or your family has become unfaithful, thoughtless or selfish. Perhaps some in-laws are breaking up their home, a husband taking too much alcohol; the children are rebellious and no longer go to church; maybe boredom, frustration and emptiness has come into your relationship with your husband or wife.

A second-rate tenor at an important opera house was singing his one big aria. At the end of it a voice from the audience cried out, 'Encore!' He was very surprised because this had never happened to him before. He sang his 'encore'. The same voice from the audience cried out again, 'Encore, Encore!' He was overwhelmed with pleasure and sang his aria again. At the end there was quietness and he waited expectantly. The voice rang out once more, 'Again, again and keep on until you get it right'.

Work at it, pray at it. Love is an answer to the discouraged parent.

Some are discouraged by their own personal failures
Dr Luis Palau, the well-known Argentinian evangelist, recently confessed to his greatest temptation. Money? Sex? Pride? No! 'My greatest temptation is just to want to give up!' How very honest. How many of us at some

time have felt like that. Elijah certainly did: 'I have had enough, Lord. . . Take my life' (I Kings 19:3). Have you ever felt like that? So 'down in the dumps' that you just want to curl up in a corner and die? What are we to do then, when we are confronted by this age-old problem?

It's a long time since old Bishop Browne of Bristol remarked, with a whimsical smile, 'Never say die till you're a lot too dead to say it'. Could this, by any chance, be a message to you? It's so easy to feel at the end of your tether, to get the conviction that it's no use trying any more or hoping again.

Well, if ever you get into that unhappy frame of mind, remember the old bishop. . . . Break through routine, shake yourself out of despair, ginger things up, hope against hope, and no matter how cruelly misfortune holds you by the throat. . .never say die!

Each year millions are spent by the NHS in providing drug therapy, shock treatment and counselling for discouraged people. Countless working days are lost through it. It is no respecter of persons. You may be discouraged for quite different reasons, such as illness, disappointment, unemployment or bereavement. Perhaps by temperament you are melancholic: you tend to look on the 'darker' side of things. Well, all these are factors that must be taken into account in seeking to diagnose it.

Failure does not necessarily mean finish in terms of spiritual experience. There are no scrap heaps of discarded Christians. As we bring our failure, hurt and bad experiences to God and give them over to Him, we discover He is the God of redemption. He is able to make all things operate for our good. He will act in forgiveness towards our repentance. He builds strength into our confessed and admitted weakness. Having identified areas of discouragement, we need now to encourage ourselves in God.

173

I imagine, no matter how depressed you were, if someone really important, like the Queen, were to phone you up and tell you how much your loyal citizenship meant to her you would feel better. God 'phones' today through His Word. Have you caught the 'gentle whisper' of His voice? (I Kings 19:12).

12. PERSIST – KEEP ON GOING FORWARD

Through tests, trials, setbacks, keep letting God lead you, guide you, use you. Many fail, for they give up for different reasons, while on God's road. Let tough times strengthen and fortify you. I like the verse –

> When you feel like giving in,
> And you're sure life's got you beat,
> Take a second breath – then try
> With more energy and heat,
> You will find, if you go to it,
> You have learnt the way to do it!

John Bunney lives opposite a bowling green. One day as a visiting party waited for their bus, John strolled over to chat with them. He noticed that an old couple, well over eighty, looked tired. So he asked them if they'd like to step over to his house for a rest and a cup of tea. Soon they were all chatting as if they'd known one another all their lives. It turned out the old man was a keen gardener, and was especially proud of his tomatoes. He'd grown them for years, and always had a grand crop.

John asked his secret. 'Well,' said the old man, 'next time you plant your tomatoes make sure you press the soil down hard on top of them. You see,' he added, 'the harder it is for the plants to come up the stronger and better they'll be.'

Soon, the bowlers' bus arrived, and John bade goodbye to his new friends. But he couldn't help thinking that the old man's advice is very like life. So often those who, like the old bowler's tomatoes, have known difficulty and setbacks, not only stand firm in life's storms but bear the better fruit.

> For every hill I've had to climb,
> For every stone that bruised my feet,
> For all the tears and sweat and grime,
> For blinding storms and burning heat,
> My heart still sings a grateful song;
> These were the things that made me strong!

Perseverance may conquer mountains. That was true of the greatest of Greek orators, Demosthenes, who, realizing his voice was weak, practised hard against the sound of the waves beating on the shore. Or Disraeli who, on his first speech in Parliament, was mocked and sneered at as a Jew. 'You will hear me yet', he shouted and, persevering, became Prime Minister.

Or take the simple courage of Robert Louis Stevenson who, when finding he had lost the power of writing with his right hand, taught himself to write with his left. Mountains are made not to be looked at but to be climbed if we have the will and the determination.

> You can't keep on? You've tried so hard?
> You've battled on so long
> This is the end. You're finished now –
> For everything's gone wrong.
> In spite of dark despair and pain
> Look up! Hold on! Begin again!

Joseph Lister, a Glasgow doctor, found the secret that doctors had searched for almost since time began. In 1864, forty-five out of every hundred patients who underwent operations did not live. Then, on an August day in 1865, a Glasgow lad called Jimmy Greenlees was brought to Lister with a badly broken leg. The doctor smiled encouragingly at the laddie as he examined him, though he knew he would almost certainly die from blood poisoning. It was the killer for which there was no known cure.

But Professor Lister had worked for years against great difficulties to find the answer. Now, despite the sneers of others, he decided to put it to the test on Jimmy. It was simple carbolic – the first antiseptic ever to be used. I cannot imagine what Lister's feeling were as he waited by the bedside of that Glasgow boy, hoping against hope. Praise be, Jimmy lived! The miracle of the antiseptic was proved beyond a shadow of doubt and the whole course of medicine was changed. *He persisted.*

Lister was showered with the highest honours. But he could never know that millions all over the world would owe their lives to him in the years to come and, as is inscribed on his grave, that 'all generations would call him blessed'.

He kept on – in faith. Those who are faithful to the end – *reap the harvest*

'If at first you don't succeed. . . .' How many of us have given up in despair after a few attempts to do something, and have marked this quotation down as nonsense? And yet, so many great people have proved it true. G.B. Shaw for instance, spent nine years in extreme poverty before he found a publisher for his books. During that time he earned only £6. But he never gave up – he always tried again. Perhaps there is a message here for you. Try again and this time, God willing, you will succeed.

On the wall near his desk a famous writer had this little verse. May I pass on these few lines to you:

Success is failure turned inside out –
The silver tint of the cloud of doubt.
And you never can tell how close you are –
It may be near when it seems so far.
So, stick to the fight when you're hardest hit.

It's when things seem worst that you mustn't quit!

It's over 225 years since Horatio Nelson was born. He was, of course, the hero of Trafalgar. But whenever I think of this famous admiral I think of the Battle of Copenhagen, in which, at one time, the engagement was so fierce that Sir Hyde Parker felt it expedient to signal Nelson to withdraw.

Nelson, however, did not wish to obey. When his attention was drawn to his superior's signal of recall, the 'bad boy' of the Navy put his telescope to his blind eye and, as he could not see the signal, he went on fighting. . .and won!

When you begin to lose heart because the going's hard, are you looking here and there for excuses to stop trying? Are you prepared to beat a retreat? Or have you something of the Nelson touch? I trust you have – and that, however long or hard the struggle, you'll keep on and on, with a grin as well as courage and determination, until you, too, win a splendid victory.

> I dare say you feel that you cannot keep on,
> And I dare say the call is so tough,
> The job is so hard or the waiting so long,
> There's nobody fit for such stuff.

> But I'm telling you – and I know this is true –
> That whatever the road you began,
> With courage and faith you will do it, for sure. . .
> If you THINK GOD can do it, YOU CAN!

13. GUARD YOUR TONGUE

G.B. Shaw said of Oscar Wilde, 'he was the greatest talker of all time'. How we should guard our tongues. I've seen such blessing lost, such talented individuals slip by the wayside due to the undisciplined tongue. Derek Bingham called the uncontrolled tongue 'the devil's bellows'! Use your words wisely.

I went into a rest room to wash my hands after a meal out with some leading pastors recently, when I saw some graffiti written over the button of the machine you dry your hands under – it read 'press this button for a tape recorded message from the Prime Minister!' *Out came hot air. . .*! There is a lot of hot air today, in the pulpit, in the church, a lot of theology, and not enough *kneeology*! We need power not just words. 'I came not to you in word only but with power', Paul was able to say. 'Guard your words.'

Sir Thomas Beecham, the great English conductor, asked about the British people and music, replied: 'the English don't care much about music, but they like the noise it makes. . .' Can that not be said about our words?

Also, *have tact*. Like the boss who said carefully to one of his employees who had been slacking a lot: 'Son, I don't know how we are going to get on without you, but starting on Monday we're going to try!'

Let your words be few unless they are positive, faith words. Paul said 'Brethren suffer exhortation. . .in a few words.' Or as the hymn says: 'Let our lips move at the impulse of thy love'. Again Scripture – 'Every idle word that men shall speak, they shall give account thereof in the day of judgement'. Sir Billy Butlin, showman, wealthy businessman, gave thousands away. Although in the public eye so much, he did not like public speeches; he used to say: 'I have only two speeches a short one – 'thank you' and a long one 'thank you very much'!

I like Proverbs 14:3 – 'the lips of the wise shall preserve thee. . .'

14. FINALLY, LOVE PEOPLE

A visitor to a certain home was intrigued to notice that a young lady spent all her time sewing; day after day she was busy with her stitches. He asked her, 'Don't you ever get tired of all this sewing?' She replied, 'Oh no, you see this is my wedding dress.' The visitor smiled and said, 'I see, it is a labour of love.'

I see my calling in life, my ministry of the Holy Spirit, as one of love, love and more love. . .a work of love, a walk of love, a life of love, a labour of love. We receive 25,000 letters yearly from the general public in our office in Chippenham, Wiltshire. Many are from desperately sick people, many write and say 'Thank you for your love for us. . . !'

In Kensington Gardens there is a bronze statue of Peter Pan. And round the pedestal on which he stands are his friends the rabbits, a snail, fairies and rats, a hare and a serious old rook. I saw the statue as the sun sank low in the sky, and I discovered that the little animals had heads and backs – not of bronze, but (as it seemed) of gold. These little creatures were so highly polished because the loving hands of tens of thousands of children had caressed them before turning away out of the Never-Never Land into a world governed by clocks and customs. And I thought, 'Love makes all things bright. . .the hard task, the poor home, the daily chores, loss of money, disappointments. Love turns the commonest stuff of life to gold!'

Love is a very abstract word until it becomes concrete and real in devotion, kindliness and compassion. A minister said, 'What am I describing?' He went on 'The anatomical juxtaposition of two oricular muscles in a state of contraction.' He had to explain it was in fact a kiss. Those words would hardly help you to know the full meaning of a kiss. We sometimes put a small X at the

179

foot of a letter to someone we love. The Christian knows it was on a real cross that love was fully revealed.

Seeing the love of Christ inspires, motivates us (Paul said the love of Christ 'drove him on') we must ever let it direct us. One of the greatest qualifications for the miraculous ministry and power bases is *to ever keep a God-like love for humanity and for others*, whether they understand us or not.

Jim married rather late in life – and Mum couldn't forgive Betty, the girl who had run off with her only son. She wasn't worthy of Jim – no girl could be. And then Jim's mother was taken ill – and without a word Jim had her brought to his own house, put to bed in the best bedroom and taken care of by Betty – who had been a nurse before she was married.

Betty went about her duties and chatted away as if Jim's mother had been the soul of kindness from the first – no recriminations, no getting her own back. . .just kindness, patience and skilled attention.

There came a Sunday evening when the patient, propped in a chair, was by the fire. In that warm glow she said, 'Betty, why have you been so kind to me?' 'Och,' said Betty, 'that's nothing. I love Jim. . .so I can't help loving you!'

The verse expresses it:

God's love is like a circle of an eternity ring,
A circle big and round,
And when you see a circle that no ending can be found
And so the love of Jesus goes eternally,
Forever and forever I know GOD LOVES ME. . .

John Fawcett was minister of the country village of Wainsgate in Yorkshire, and though his church and stipend were small, the deep bond between him and his flock more than made up for both. Then one day an invitation arrived asking him to preach at St Paul's Cathedral in London – for word of his good work had

180

reached the bishop himself. Well, he did preach at St Paul's – and so successfully that he was offered the pulpit of a great London church which would bring him fame and comfort. It was like an opportunity from heaven itself – and he accepted.

At length the time came for him to leave Wainsgate. The waggons were loaded and ready to leave. But when Fawcett stepped outside the door he found that the whole village had gathered to bid a last goodbye to their beloved minister – and he knew then he could never leave his faithful folk. He loved them so much.

He ordered the men to unload the furniture and take it back inside his manse – and that evening, as he sat at his desk in the old, familiar study, he realized how right he had been to stay. So before he went to bed, he wrote a prayer and it has become a hymn that is sung the world over. 'Blest be the tie that binds our hearts in Jesus's love'.

In the midst of misunderstanding, ill-will, even corruption and hatred, we must see, look for and express God's *LOVE*. The verse goes –

> In a crazy world where so much is wrong,
> Let's try to find the things that cheer;
> There's the happy smile and the well-loved song
> There's a garden at set of sun,
> Stars that shine in the night above. . .
> And the big, strong faith that, when all is done,
> Behind life's ills is God's great love.

May we have the desire of the little child talking one day to her Auntie, 'Suppose you could have a wish,' Aunt Ida suggested 'what would you ask for?' Little Brenda replied: 'An old doll.' 'Wouldn't you rather have a new one?' Brenda shook her head, 'Oh, no,' said she, 'I'd like an old doll. New dolls get loved a lot, but old dolls are thrown on one side and get forgotten. I'd like an old doll who wanted somebody to love her – and I'd love her and love her and love her!'

On hearing a very graphic description of the crucifixion a young boy cried out, 'If God had been there He would not have let them do it!' Then he heard a simple talk about God's love and the meaning of the cross and cried out again, 'Oh good, He was there all the time!'

God wants us to show His love all the time to hard, Christ-rejecting, loveless folk.

I had a wonderful holiday in the Scottish Isles, in particular on Skye, a few years ago. If you ever visit there you must go on a boat trip to the Isle of Mull – there on the cliffs you will see the great Bible text. The story goes that a father on a visit to Mull was strolling along the cliff-top path with his little daughter, when the child tripped and tumbled over the precipice. With fear clutching his heart, the father raced down the path to the beach, telling himself no one could survive such a fall. Yet, to his amazement, he found his daughter not only alive but only slightly hurt. That day, after taking his girl home, he went back to the cliff face with paint and brush and at the spot where she had fallen he painted the text, 'God is Love', for he believed only a miracle had saved his child. Then he asked the crew of the mailboat to promise to renew the message from time to time, so that all who came and went would see it.

Today, years later, the men of the mailboat are still keeping their word, for the message is still there, proclaiming a father's faith to all who pass.

God loves us so much, we must endeavour to love and rescue others from their sins and bring them to His Love as he desires us to.

It seems that when Prince Albert died, Queen Victoria took her grief to Balmoral, and there, in the isolation of her position, she remembered him.

Then, by some strange chance, word reached her that the husband of a woman in a nearby cottage had died.

The Queen immediately wrapped herself in her cloak, ordered a coach to be brought round, and quietly left the castle. Soon, she was at the house, and, almost unnoticed lifted the latch and went in. But word of her arrival did get around the village; and when the Queen left, neighbours crowded into the wee room with the same question on their lips. 'What did she say?', they asked. 'She didna say anything', came the calm reply. 'She cam' in; she sat doon beside me; she took my hand. And we baith wept.'

Truly, two women whose lives and ways were poles apart and yet the great Queen shared her silent deep love.

My ministry has produced many bona-fide miracles of divine healing, medically-substantiated cases of startling cures through prayer for thousands of people. I have won over 100,000 souls and established some fifty churches. *But if I had helped only one soul in heaven through my efforts, if I had helped, encouraged, loved, shown kindness to and inspired just a few people through all my service for Jesus, it would be worth it.*

If I could only say the words of this rhyme, these lines, my calling, my life has been fulfilled:

> If some person may be,
> Stronger for the strength I bring,
> Sweeter for the songs I sing,
> Happier for the path I tread,
> Lighter for the light I shed,
> Richer for the gifts I give,
> Purer for the life I live,
> Nobler for the death I die,
> *Not in vain, have I been here. . .*

God wants you to become a candidate for the supernatural. To stand in the victory Jesus Christ has won for us. To prosper the work of your hands, to clothe yourself in the armour of light. The twentieth-century Church and our desperate world need badly some shining faces and some powerful deliverers, like Deborah, Gideon, Esther, Daniel; like Luther, Wesley, Whitfield, Evan Roberts, Billy Nicholson, The Jeffrey Brothers, Smith Wigglesworth. . .seek the qualifications to manifest the miraculous.

As Winston Churchill said – 'Cost, sorrow will be the companion of our journey, hardship, constancy and valour our shield. We must be undaunted, inflexible.'

Paul reminds us. 'Since we receive a Kingdom which cannot be shaken, let us show to God an acceptable service with reverence and awe' (Hebrews 12:28; NASB).

PART THREE

Light and Darkness

Light and Darkness –
A sermon given by Melvin Banks

They grope in darkness without light. . .(but) . . .
The Lord shall be to (them) an Everlasting light
                                        Job 12: 25 and Isaiah 60: 20

A minister was travelling by bus late one Saturday night. It wasn't what you could call an enjoyable trip, for a party of men had joined the bus and it was obvious from their shouting and singing they had had more than their fair share to drink.

Mr Barkham couldn't help feeling sorry for the young conductress and, as a fellow passenger remarked, her job was hard enough without having to put up with that kind of behaviour.

Just then, however, the bus stopped. As the minister watched, the conductress calmly pushed her way through the men and stretched out her arm to one of the passengers. A few seconds later, she came back down the bus leading a man to the platform.

All eyes turned to watch as she left the bus and led the man across the road. . .he was blind. She became his eyes, his light.

The wonderful thing was that by the time she returned, you could have heard a pin drop on the bus. There was no more shouting and singing, and when the pastor reached his stop, he paused to murmur a word of thanks to the conductress.

By one kindly gesture, she had achieved more than any ordering or pleading would have done – simply by being *A light to one in the dark!*

Our world lies in Darkness – People have no light! No illumination! No insight! No revelation!

A TV show in Britain some time ago showed, at the end of the programme, the compère bringing on all the acts and cast to the stage before the audience. They all acted as if blindfolded and went around in circles, bumping into one another, pushing one another, laughing and each one saying aloud, 'I am lost, I am lost'; it was pitiful, as the audience roared with laughter. How true it was, blind, purposeless, wandering, lost without light or direction. A text says, 'the light shines in the darkness and the darkness has not overcome it'.

The Word says again – *'Ye were darkness but now are ye light'*. When the great Scots writer was a boy, Robert Louis Stevenson lived in Edinburgh. He was about six years of age and a very sickly child. One night as he was about to go to bed he peeped through the window and excitedly called his nurse, for he saw the old lamp lighter coming down the street with his long pole igniting the street lamps: 'Look, nurse!' he cried. 'Look at that man who is going down the street making *holes in the dark!'*

So Jesus came to make a hole in the darkness of man's night.

1. We see first the darkness of man's personal nature

Isaiah said – the people 'wait for light but. . .walk in darkness' (Isaiah 59:9) and Paul said – 'they have the understanding darkened' (Ephesians 4:18). Again, they 'grope in the dark without light' – Job declared (Job 12:25).

George Fox said society was covered in an 'ocean of darkness'. The Bible speaks of the 'unfruitful works of darkness'; again of the 'rulers of the darkness of this world'; it tells us to 'cast off the works of darkness', and again it says of us personally – 'ye were sometimes

188

darkness' and 'ye walk in darkness, lie and do not speak the truth' (1 John 1:6).

In New York during the great power workers' strike a number of years ago, the whole city was plunged into darkness, the crime rate reached an all-time high. Even respectable people who had never been in trouble with the law before went looting, stealing, and pilfering. The darkness had brought the worst out of people; *darkness is a personification of sin and evil.* One spot of darkness can affect the whole of life, one jealousy, one spirit of pride, uncleanness, one gossiping tongue can affect many lives for ill. One sin can sink a sinner into hell. One sin can mar a whole life, one hole can sink a ship, one slate off a roof can bring in wet and damp, into the whole building. A big game hunter had many a close shave, a lion jumped him, a man-eating tiger scratched his face before he managed to shoot it and he wrote a best-seller telling of his amazing escapades. Then, years later when he was on a farm in Illinois, USA, he was scratched by a farmyard cat and died the next day!

Recently an entire city underground transport system suddenly stopped. Men and women sweated in darkness. Children panicked. Everyone wondered what the fault could be. It turned out to be a Coca Cola tin which had short-circuited the system! A DC10 plunged to earth from French air space and lives were tragically cut off. The reason? A faulty aircraft door. The Titanic sliced into an iceberg and as she sank the cry for help went out from her radio operator. Another ship only ten miles away failed to respond. The reason? Its radio operator was asleep. Over a thousand lives were lost.

Blondin was known as the 'Conqueror of Niagara'. He even walked over on a tightrope pushing a wheelbarrow with a man in it! But finally he died when he slipped upon his doormat, walking out of his own front door in Ealing, London! We can be killed by a small thing as much as by a big thing. A little darkness can cloud one's life, a little sin can destroy and mar our happiness.

Jesus warned – 'Take heed that the light which is in thee be not darkness'.

The Bible says of the sinful – 'They shall never see light'; and Isaiah declared – *they behaved immoral, unclean and in evil ways* 'because there is no light in them. . . .' (Isaiah 8:20).

As Masefield put it regarding our personal sin and darkness – 'My soul has many dark decaying rooms hung with the ragged areas of the past. . .'

The Rev Foster Hall visited Mrs Gordon, who is 82 – a cheery and independent old soul. When the minister arrived, she was sitting by her gleaming fireside watching her daughter and a neighbour doing the cleaning. When the house was shining like a new pin they went outside to clean the window. But they found that neither of them could reach the top panes.

What was to be done? The minister promptly took off his jacket, climbed on a chair and did the job with a chamois.

When he came back into the room, Mrs Gordon expertly surveyed the window. 'Not so bad', was her verdict. Then her eyes twinkled merrily. 'But then,' she added, 'it's a minister's job to let the light in'.

But how true – it is the task of every Christian to let the light in! Also to take the light of the Gospel to all men that they might believe and leave their hideous darkness to find the light of the world.

Transformation at a stroke

An artist drew a picture of a winter scene; trees heavily laden with snow, a dreary desolate home and a starless night sky. Then with a stroke of a yellow crayon, he put a light in one window of the house. The effect was striking. The entire scene was transformed into a vision of comfort and good cheer.

190

The coming of Christ did that to a dark, dreary world as He does to every one who opens his life to the Saviour. He is indeed the light of the world, the master transformer.

Luke calls Jesus 'a light to lighten the gentiles' (the non-Jew). Darkness evaporates when faced with the light, as the Psalmist said – 'the entrance of thy word gives light' (Psalm 119:130). Again. . . 'Thy word is a lamp unto my way and a light unto my path' (Psalm 119:105). So we must go out as believers, and as Peter said – 'become a light shining in a dark place' (2 Peter 1:19).

Years ago a curate in West Yorkshire told the story of a small boy who was taken to look round an ancient church by his father who had been trying to explain what a saint was. Together they gazed up at a stained glass window depicting a saint, but the little lad was not at all impressed, until suddenly the sun shone through the window illuminating the jewelled colours and making it 'come alive'. 'Oh, now I see', cried the boy. 'A saint is someone the sun shines through.' God's Son wants to shine with the divine light through us – He said, 'While ye have light, believe in the light.'

2. Secondly there is the darkness of death

A minister took a funeral service at a crematorium. As usual there was a hymn book left in readiness for him, but the minister was mildly surprised to see that it was not the copy he was accustomed to using. He found, in fact, that the hymn book was no longer in use – because of a missing page.

And why was the page missing? The explanation is simple, yet telling. The page contained the hymn 'Abide with me', and it had been used so often during funeral services that it had worn out long before the rest of the hymn book. Isn't it a striking thought that in time of grief, all of us, rich and poor, young or old, turn to the timeless promise of Francis Lyte's great hymn? 'I fear no foe, with Thee at hand to bless. . . .'

The Brixham, Devon, minister who died saying – 'light, joy. . .peace' indeed shed light and victory in face of death through his triumphant faith in Christ, his Master. However, the people of this world do not have such a light or hope. When Bertrand Russell died he said. . . 'there is darkness without *and now there is darkness within*'.

People are scared of dying. Muhammed Ali said – 'I am scared of no one, but I am scared of dying; no one wants to die. . .' George Bernard Shaw did a survey of death and said he arrived at the interesting conclusion that 'one out of one dies'. David said in Psalm 89:48 – 'What man can lie and not see death, or save himself from the power of the grave?'

People wonder about this age-old question

Even children ask about death. In the book *Children's letters to God* one charming, moving letter says –

Dear God

What is it like when a person dies? Nobody will tell me, I just want to know. I don't want to die yet.

Your friend
Mike

When we prepare to die we prepare to live. Job said – 'man's days are determined. . .with thee, thou [GOD] has appointed his bounds, that he cannot pass. . .'

An old Welsh miner lay dying, a dear Christian most of his life. 'Can you hear the music? I never heard such music in my life. . .' Then he was gone. There was no music, only silence in the room. He had heard *the heavenly music welcoming him home*.

192

There's spot which I hear of. It's a cemetery, quiet and still. Many people visit it. . .but I was told of a very special visitor. Apparently he lives some distance away, but from time to time he faithfully makes the journey in tribute to someone he loves. Even in the dark of winter he comes. Then he carries a torch, which lights his way to the grave he knows so well. For a few moments it shines brightly on a headstone – then he turns away and the hallowed spot is dark once more. Who is he? A son visiting a mother? A husband turning over memories, still green, of a companion on life's way? A father remembering a little one still dear to him? No one knows. But I admire him – *hope, light – burns not only in his hand, but in his heart.*

Of course there is the funny side of dying too, like the visit to the graveyard and the sometimes amusing stones one reads such as these I noted –

> Erected to the memory of John McFarlane
> drowned in the waters of Leith
> by a few affectionate friends. . .

and this one –

> Here lies Andrew McPherson
> who was a peculiar person,
> stood six feet two without his
> shoe
> and he was slew, at Waterloo. . .!

An Irish coroner declared recently 'there are people dying this year who never died before'. Woody Allen, the famous American comedian, when asked if he was frightened to die, replied, 'No, I'm not, but I don't want to be there when it happens!' John Wesley the famous evangelist sat in a waggon and read the Bible to a highwayman on the way to be hanged. He replied,

'I am not afraid to die, I have faced death as a highway man hundreds of times; but I am afraid of what lies beyond.'

Even many great men feared death. Napoleon said shortly before his death: 'I die before my time and my body will be given back to the earth, to become the food of worms; such is the fate which so soon awaits the great Napoleon.'

Sir Walter Raleigh wrote – 'The dark and silent grave shuts up the story of our days'.

I know a woman in her eighties, a frail body with a serene face that peeps above the bedclothes. With the courage given to so many old folk, she calmly faces the knowledge that she will soon be blind. Gradually, her sight has been failing, and with cheerful resignation she has been preparing herself for what lies ahead. She knows she stands at the crossroads of light and dark, and it has no terrors for her. Patiently she is memorizing everything she holds dear. . .the faces of her sisters; the first light of morning; the words of her favourite hymn that have been a comfort in difficult times. . .and many other treasures that now mean more than ever to her. Truly, I salute this gallant old lady who carries her own lantern on the journey into the dark.

This good lady is preparing herself for that final hour and day when she faces our darkest enemy. But she has found that the power and presence of Jesus sheds light, immortality and power to vanquish the darkness, as the old verse goes –

it takes its terror from the grave,
and gilds the bed of death with light.

A man of God was asked to visit a dying husband. As he entered the bedroom where the man lay, his wife said, 'He cannot hear you, he is deaf; he cannot see you, he is blind. *But I just want him to get a breath of you.*'

194

God wants to breathe into us life, certainty, assurance for the future.

Edward Thomas, the great First-World-War Wiltshire poet, wrote so aptly: 'a mouthful of earth to remedy all. . .down to a poor man of any sort, down to a King. . .wondering where he shall journey, O where . . .O where?'

Rupert Brooke expressed it: 'this life cannot be all there is beyond the space and time. . .in that heaven shall be their wish. . . .' Christ conquered death and hell, took away the sting, the shame, the fear and darkness for ever. *Do not fear, all is well, you are bound for the eternal city of everlasting light, where there is no night there. . .if you have Christ's glorious light shining in your heart!*

I love the story of Corrie ten Boom's witness in Holland during World War II. Who could fail to be challenged and encouraged by her testimony and courage in the Ravensbruck concentration camp?

There, in the pit of evil and darkness, she started a prayer group and Bible study. She wrote:

"Waifs clustered round a blazing fire, we gathered about it – holding out our hearts to its warmth and light. The blacker the night around us grew, the brighter and more beautiful burned the Word of God as we read: 'In all these things we have complete victory through him who loved us. . .'"

No matter what darkness of temptation we face, or overwhelming sense of despair and evil, we can draw on His risen power to lead us through to victory. The seal is broken, corrupt authority is defeated. In Christ we have the victory. In His power we must learn to live it day by day.

The fierce reality of their role in the story came home to me when I visited St Peter's in Gallicantu last August. In the basement of that church is the site where many believe Jesus was scourged. The whip marks and whipping posts still stand from antiquity.

As I stood in that dark dungeon, the agony of His physical and mental torture came home to me in a new and powerful way. Those soldiers were the instrument of suffering. As they slumbered outside the tomb that morning, they were the victors.

It seemed that suffering was triumphant, the cruel torment of the soldiers had been victorious. Christ was defeated. But nothing could be further from the truth! For soon He burst victorious from the tomb.

> Up from the grave he arose,
> With a mighty triumph o'er his foes,
> He arose a victor from the dark domain,
> And he lives forever with his saints to reign,
> He arose! Hallelujah! Christ arose!

And when he rose again, what happened to the soldiers? They ran away! The symbol of suffering was overcome, defeated and powerless. Christ had overcome the power of suffering.

We shall all die one day, unless the Lord comes first. There is suffering in this life, but God said also – '*I am the Lord that healeth thee. . . .*' God has new, energizing, liberating, healing power, to extend life, bring comfort, give supernatural strength. Many Christians are not living in or enjoying all God saved them for. Multitudes of sinners do not know God is a miraculous God, who can save from ill-health, disease and death. He has all power in heaven and on earth. God has a wider purpose for the world. He is giving to us in our Crusade services manifestations of power that deny all human explanations. *Christ is our all-in-all. . . .we constantly see him giving miracles of healing! Miracles of changed lives! Miracles of cleansed sinners*! . . . . the work of *one man* our beautiful Lord Jesus. . . .the wonders are His. *Jesus is front page news in these* great campaigns *of ours* across the U.K. The world is sick. He is the great healer and miracle worker. Healing, new health, miracles are ingredients of the message – Gods special offer in the Gospel. The power of God is hovering over us, in this meeting today! . . .people are dying in their millions in the darkness, as Job said – 'from the city men groan, and the souls of the wonded cry out' (Job 24:12; NASB). People are desolate, diseased, full of deep hurts, painful and bleeding. Job said – 'they rebel agains the light. . .they ally themselves with the terrors of darkness. . .' (Job 24:13, 16–17; NASB) *We must bring* them the glorious New Testament message – God has enough power to save and heal the whole world.

He is the ressurrection and the Life. He smashed the 'last enemy': death and it has become merely a shadow to the true believer. He is the miraculous, all-powerful one. *He is* health, life, ressurrection. Certainty for the future. *In a sense the true believer never dies!*

A few years ago I conducted a funeral for my Uncle Percy – he was in the Royal Flying Corps, the forerunner of the Royal Air Force, in World War I, in France. A brave and good man. Among the hymns we sang for him:

We're marching to Zion; beautiful, beautiful Zion;
We're marching onward to Zion; the beautiful City of God.'

We know His risen power in our dying as well as in our living. As we face death we face it in His resurrection power. In the victory He won we inherit a life eternal and imperishable.

Hear the words of dying men of great faith –

Luther – 'God is the Lord, with whom we escape death'.

John Knox – 'Die in Christ, and the flesh need not fear.'

Richard Baxter – 'I have pain but there is peace'

The Rev Augustus Toplady (who wrote 'Rock of Ages')
– 'I am enjoying heaven already'!

Sir Walter Raleigh, as he stood on the scaffold about
to die handed his pocket watch to the executioner and
said: 'Take my timepiece. . .I am now dealing with
eternity'.

Long years ago – so runs the old tale – there was a very
small courtyard in a big town. In that courtyard lived a
dozen folk or so, mostly elderly; and they complained
bitterly because there was not a glimmer of light in the
courtyard after nightfall. Time and time again somebody
tripped over the rough cobblestones or bumped his or
her head against a projecting stone in a wall – for there
was nothing to do on winter nights but grope one's
way along a dark passage and then fumble across the
courtyard till one found one's own door. Somebody
living in the courtyard once dared to suggest that all the
inhabitants of the little cottages should club together to
buy a lamp which was to be hung at the end of the passage
– but they didn't want to go to such expense.

At last, one of the cottagers died and an old lady came
to live in the courtyard. She, too, discovered within
a week how shockingly dark the spot was and how
dangerous it was, by night, to go even as far as the
communal pump. So she moved her table lamp from its
place near the fire to a place near her window – and she
pulled aside the curtains. Her room was well-enough lit
with the lamp in that position – and her window banished
the darkness of the courtyard and guided all who came
along the passage.

Eventually all her neighbours followed her example –
all putting lamps in their windows; and thus the darkest
courtyard became by night the brightest in all the city.
So, with the flaming light of Jesus in you – you can show
others the way through the darkness into that wonderful
Heaven. The Bible says: 'For the law of the spirit of life

in Christ Jesus, hath made me free from the law of sin and death.'

Thank God, Jesus 'brought life and immortality to light through the Gospel' (2 Timothy 1:10). We look not for the grave but for the glory. Death has lost its darkness for the believer! As Samuel said, 'The Lord will lighten my darkness', and Isaiah added, 'The people in darkness. . .that dwell in the land of the shadow, upon them hath the light shined'. (Isaiah 9:2) The believer has light and heaven to look forward to.

A little girl had been to Sunday School for the first time and was asked by her mother how it compared with the day school. 'Oh! I like it much better', she said. 'There are no exams there, and at the end you go to heaven instead of secondary school.'

3. Thirdly there is the darkness of trial and trouble

People of this world, leaders, many of the finest of people in society, have lost hope. They see only darkness covering the earth. For instance, the Duke of Edinburgh quoted in *Woman's Own* a few years ago said: 'I have nightmares about the sort of world the next generation is going to have to live in. The older I get the more cynical I get. . .I think things are going to get worse.'

Rudyard Kipling, describing another troubled time in our history, adequately expressed these present times that face our world in those apt words:

> This is the midnight, let no star delude us.
> Dawn is very far,
> This is the tempest long foretold,
> Slow to make head – but sure to hold.

We all have troubles in life. Jeremiah said in that epic poem: 'My eye is filled with tears, my heart is troubled. . .behold and see if there is any sorrow, like my sorrow which has been brought upon me.' Winston Churchill said: 'a man can stand up to almost any thing, but he cannot stand up against uncertainty. . .' People are disappointed with life all around us. When people have everything they are sad, and when they fail to get what they want they worry, and are anxious–darkness indeed. The old legend says that a teardrop fell into the river and floated down with another. They engaged in conversation. One said, 'Who are you?' She replied, 'The teardrop who lost her man to another'. She then asked, 'Who are you though?' and the other teardrop answered, 'I'm the one who *got him*!!'

Once upon a time there was an ant that grumbled away for all he was worth. He had to carry a piece of straw nearly an inch long, which was pretty much the same as if you had to stagger along with a log on your shoulder. Believe me, that ant was fed up with life. All he could do was to creep across a desert of concrete until cruel Fate brought him to a crack. There was no getting across that crack – not even *without* the straw, let alone with it. So there the ant paused. . .until a thought struck him.

Suddenly he saw that his trouble might be a blessing! He laid that straw across the crack in the concrete, walked over it and safely reached the far side. Perhaps some of our troubles and sufferings might be turned to good account if only we began looking at them from a new angle.

See your troubles in God's light – from his angle. God's light dispels the darkness of failure, fear, depression, sadness that would come upon us

4. Then we see the end of Darkness.

In George Orwell's famous, almost prophetic, book, *1984* there is one line of hope. In the appalling darkness of that book, as the hero Winston Smith takes his stand against the evil anti-Christ figure Big Brother, he exclaims with hope – 'One day we shall meet in that place where there is no darkness!'

A father was bringing up his little son alone, due to the death of the mother. His little one would not sleep alone, so he had a small bed put in the corner of his own bedroom. The boy never liked the dark. Finally one night after retiring himself and persuading the little fellow it was time to put the light out, the boy called out in the dark, 'You still there, Dad?' 'Yes, my son' came the reply. A few minutes later, 'Are you still awake, Dad?' 'Yes, my son.' Then a long silence and Dad thought he had now gone off to sleep. Finally came a cry: 'Dad, *are you looking my way in the darkness?*' Many people have forgotten God altogether in the darkness of our world, many Christians have to be reminded also, that He is still watching us and *'looking our way'* even in the deep night of this world today.

In the days of the old sailing ships, a terrible storm came. It looked as if this ship would be surely lost. It was driven out of control seemingly, water poured over its decks, the sail was broken. It was swept along by high seas and fierce winds at their mercy. The passengers lay holding on deep in the ship's interior, but all seemed lost. Finally, after hours of danger, one of the crew crawled along the length of the hold and lifted the hatch. The storm was still very bad and the darkness of the elements lit up only by heavy lightning. After peeping at the events above, the man ran down to the passengers and announced all would be well. Many asked, 'why do you say that? The storm is still increasing'. He replied: *I saw the captain's face and he was smiling. . . .'* He knew *his captain* and if he was smiling in the dark then all would be well. . . The Captain in his great knowledge of the sea and in his wisdom could see the storm was soon coming to an end and the darkness would soon give way to *the light of dawn. . .*

Remember: Jesus is your light in the time of the darkness of sin, death, trouble and trial.

When Winter comes, with the shorter days and the longer nights ahead, remember what Sir Harry Lauder used to say about the dark? All his life he had a soft spot for Leerie-light-the-lamp. Even as a child he used to watch at the window for Leerie coming along, his pole on his shoulder. . .and how thrilling it was to see the darkness behind him giving place to one halo of light after another, till a long row of lights reached from end to end of the street.

It was fun, Sir Harry tells us, seeing Old Leerie, the lamp-lighter going by – always plodding into the darkness, always leaving a trail of light behind. As the years went by, Sir Harry realized there was more to it than that – it was a challenge to him to light a lamp wherever there was darkness. And isn't that your job and mine? As we travel through this world, darkened by sorrow, what a glorious opportunity we have of lighting lamps in other people's lives and thus, when we come to the end of the road, leaving a trail of light behind us!

It says in Colossians, God hath 'delivered us from the domain of darkness and translated us into the Kingdom of His Dear Son'. He is the Light of Life 'in Him there is no darkness at all'. Doubts are vanished, trials eased, frustrations ended, oppressions conquered. . .we are going to that city, *'where the Lamb is the light thereof. . .'*

A friend tells me that just below the light switch in his bedroom hangs a card. It's about the last thing his eye rests on before he turns out the light and gets into bed. On the card are three words – 'Tomorrow's all yours.' And my friend assures me this motto has had a lot to do with his good life.

Over the years he's had many a hard fight, many a disappointment, many a defeat. Often at the end of the day he's felt he'd made a mess of things. And then he's seen this card with its message of hope and challenge – today's been wasted but tomorrow was all his, all his to use to try again and do better. To live in the light and lessons of today's mistakes. He found that the dark failures soon ended, as tomorrow he lived again in the light.

The Scripture says: 'The path of the just, the righteous, the pure, the forgiven ones, is as the *shining light*, that shineth more and more until the perfect day (in heaven).'

5. Finally, we see darkness and light is eternal

In Scripture Isaiah the prophet declared that, for the believer, 'The Lord shall be to thee everlasting light' (60:70).

But the unrepentant, the indifferent, the apathetic and the hard-hearted it says, shall finally 'be reserved in everlasting chains under darkness. . .forever' . . .and again they are – 'reserved (in) blackness forever' (Jude 6 and 13).

Every foggy night, a light shines out over the moor that lies between Falkirk and Slamannan. It burns in a little cottage off the main road. . .and it burns for a boy called Robert. Robert lived in the cottage, and went to school at Falkirk. The bus that brought him back stopped at the main road, and from there he walked up the lonely, twisting lane to his home.

Often the moor was foggy, and Robert's mother lit a paraffin lamp and put it in the window to guide him. He could see it through the fog. Even when Robert grew up and went to work at the brickworks, the lamp shone for him. Then came the war and he was called to the Army. But before he went away, his mother made him a promise. 'I'll still put your light in the window', she said. 'Then if you come home on a foggy night, it'll be there to guide you.' Unhappily, Robert didn't come home. . . In 1944 he was reported missing, believed dead. But if ever you travel over the moor on a foggy night you will still see Robert's lamp shining. For, like the love his mother holds for him, it burns on, clear and bright and enduring.

I cannot think of a more moving scene than that which takes place at the memorial in Melbourne, Australia, where lies the body of an unknown soldier. The vast memorial is in the shape of an arch and stands reflected in the diamond waters of a pool. When the arch was built, the designers left the memorial in darkness, apart from a tiny slit in the roof. And they planned it so that the sun, which shines all the year round, would send a slender shaft of light through that slit only at the eleventh hour of the eleventh day of the eleventh month. Only then, when the world stops in its stride, does the light fall on the Rock of Remembrance.

Then Jesus said unto them, 'Yet a little while is the light with you. Walk while ye have the light, lest darkness come upon you: for he that walketh in darkness knoweth not whither he goeth.'

The world lies in darkness, when Jesus seeks you – receive his light and live in it always!

Jesus said – 'I AM THE LIGHT OF THE WORLD . . .'

Recently we had the fiftieth anniversary of the radio broadcast of the words of our local Somerset poet, Minnie Hoskins from Warmley, Bristol. I refer to the first wartime broadcast message of a King of England. He quoted from the words that were to become world-famous, written by an unknown poetess, Miss Hoskins, the little Born Again lady, whose words got into the hands of King George VI, who used them to inspire fifty-one million fellow Britons and millions of others in other parts of the world. Europe stood about to fall under the appalling darkness and evil of Nazism. For

Britain it was to be her darkest hour, she stood virtually alone – or was about to do so – with her Empire, against the greatest evil and most powerful war machine ever seen up to that time.

Fear gripped the nation as we were outgunned, outnumbered unprepared for the massive evil onslaught of the enemy. Then came that poem that helped ignite a nation's faith and hope, one that older folk have never forgotten at that dark awful evil hour –

I said to the man that stood at the gate of the year –
'Give me a light that I may go out into the unknown'.
And he replied, '*Put your hand into the hand of God. That is better than light, and surer than a known way. . .*'

Jesus said, 'He that followeth me shall have the light of life. . . (John 9:5) Only Christ can give us true guidance, peace, tranquillity, freedom, assurance, happiness and LIGHT. . .

The little village of Ecclesmachan in Scotland lost a precious friend when they lost their minister. I never met Mr Pinkerton, but I learned from others how for thirty years he served his people.

No task was too little or too great for him. If he found anyone in need of comfort and shelter, he took them into his manse and fed them and cared for them. And he faced the blows of life like a man. One Sunday morning he unveiled a memorial to those who fell in the war. Among the names he read out was that of his only son. But, unfalteringly, his strong voice read on, despite the anguish in his heart.

Now he is gone. How appropriate it is that carved in stone above his manse door are these words:

In casting light into the dark places, my own life is burning away, but the crown of life remaineth.

God's light is eternal.

Scripture says 'Then shall the righteous shine forth as the sun in the kingdom of their Father.'

We must repent. . .turn from our sins and do them no more. Let God break the power of the law of sin and death, and lift that curse that is upon you. . .

Have faith in the finished work of Calvary, in the Blood shed on the Cross. There is omnipotence, light, pardon, power, release, forgiveness through the blood-stream of Calvary.

Receive Jesus, with a broken heart, with weeping and sorrow over your sin, come in awe and the fear of the lord.

God is preparing a people in this dark world to be a light to lighten up the whole earth.

God is getting a people ready for the Coming of the Lord.

I urge you to return to Jesus Christ, the 'Shepherd and Bishop of your souls' and the everlasting light!

It was in 1943 in Sicily, and Mr Keillor had been helping in the burial of many soldiers. The loss of so many good and gallant friends in one day had left his spirit utterly desolate. And when he turned from the last grave in the evening, he found himself crying – 'Can I still believe there is a God?'

All round him the ground was black and shell-blasted. He stumbled and fell into a shell hole. It was black there, too, but at the very bottom of the hole he saw one tiny shoot of green grass. As Mr Keillor lay still, he seemed to hear a voice which said: 'Oh, where is your faith?'

That was the miracle which gave him the fresh hope he needed to carry on.

For in the darkness he saw life, new creation, light coming out of blackness, hope out of despair, *new life out of death. So light, power, God's life conquers darkness*; and so we step out into *eternal life with Jesus*.

Say *'Yes' today to the invitation*. As the prophet put it – *'Come, let us walk in the light of the lord'*. . . (Isaiah 2:5)
The old statement goes – 'you may not be able to reach the light, but you can put the switch on!' You can have faith, you can use it, you can live a fuller life in God's light. Your dedication, surrender, commitment, love, actions and faith can help to throw new light on the earth's dark patches. The little boy was playing with his toys; it was getting dusk, and soon he could hardly see the game he was lost in. Realizing this, he called out – *'Hi! MUM, PUT THE DARK OUT!'* So the Children of God are called to live in His light, so as to PUT OUT the darkness of the world's fears, dilemmas, terrors, decadence and uncertainties.

THE GREAT GOD OF LIGHT NEVER LOST A BATTLE – let us join him, and not rest until bathed with spiritual light, we climb the hill of God, and SHINE FOR JESUS, SHINE till the whole world resounds with praises to THE LIGHT OF THE WORLD. For soon the whole resounds with praises to the feet of OUR LORD, JESUS CHRIST – who is the 'God who hath showed us light' (Psalm 118: 27). Until that day, we must obey Jesus, who commanded us: 'Whatever I tell you . . . speak in the light and preach on the housetops' (Matthew 10:27). One day, Spurgeon was pointing out the work of an old lamplighter to a friend, as he broke up the darkness with his pockets of light, and left lighted lamps shining behind him, finally disappearing over the hill. THAT'S WHAT I WANT TO LEAVE BEHIND WHEN I GO OVER THE HILL AND AM SEEN NO MORE – A WORLD LIT UP WITH THE GOSPEL LIGHT! What about YOU?

SAY 'YES' TO THIS INVITATION TODAY. As the prophet put it – *"Come, let us walk in the light of the Lord"*

(Isaiah 2:5)

MAKE UP YOUR MIND TO LOVE HIM AND
WALK WITH HIM ALL THE DAYS OF YOUR
LIFE.